Sarah Watkins has given teachers, paren[...] heartfelt guide to nature connection. Th[...] next generation of children and families.

Richard Louv, author of Last Child in the Woods *and* Vitamin N

The most brilliant, easy to read and engaging book on outdoor learning and play I have ever read. Packed full of rich anecdotes and solid research, it is an indispensable guide for educators everywhere.

Mike Fairclough, author of Wild Thing *and Headmaster of West Rise Junior School, winner of the TES School of the Year*

A must-read. This remarkable book is an essential read for anyone who values outdoor play and well-being. It is packed full of practical, accessible ideas and strategies underpinned by the latest research. I thoroughly enjoyed reading it and reflecting on how to support nature connectedness in our settings. *Outdoor Play for Healthy Little Minds* reminds us that 'the best classroom and the richest cupboard are roofed only by the sky.'

Anthony Hadfield, ex-headteacher and founder of Head into the Wild

This book is lovingly filled with the joy of play. Packed full of useful suggestions, examples of practice and insightful comments from the children themselves, this is a wonderful book. Sarah combines her deep knowledge of children and their capacity to learn with a clear rationale of the ways in which play builds cognitive understanding, emotional and physical development and social connection. I recommend this book highly for all those who seek to understand children further and celebrate the wonders of childhood.

Dame Alison Peacock, Chief Executive at the Chartered College of Teaching and Honorary Fellow of Queen's College, Cambridge

This wonderful book shows how play develops skills that lead to balanced, resilient people. Parents, teachers and all of us who work with children will find valuable ways to look at the world through fresh eyes.

Dr Simon Lennane, GP and Mental Health GP Lead,
Herefordshire Clinical Commissioning Group (CCG)

This is a delightful and very special gem of a book! Warm, personal, thought-provoking, extensively researched and jam packed with brilliant and practical ideas for outdoor learning and play. I have admired Sarah's knowledge, wisdom and expertise for a long time and in this book Sarah gives us the know-how and confidence to optimise our school grounds and approach to play to develop imagination, creativity, well-being, language skills, resilience, and promote co-existence, equity and inclusion. I have learned a lot, this is a must read guide for any early years practitioner and primary school leaders. I will be buying several copies for my school!

Rae Snape, Headteacher and National Leader of Education

What a jewel; this book is filled to bursting with stunning photographs of real examples of outdoor play and learning in action to inform and inspire, with 'time to reflect' opportunities throughout to support ongoing practitioner CPD – something which is essential. Sarah demonstrates that valuable outdoor play and learning opportunities are everywhere and can be achieved easily, for all our children, by thinking creatively, listening to and following children's interests, using simple resources and by tapping into what Mother Nature gives us. Definitely on the reading list for my early years educator trainees to support outdoor play, knowledge and practice.

Helin Taylor-Greenfield, early years Lecturer (FE), NNEB,
Pearson, and LBWF Teaching Award Winner

Sarah Watkins has written one of the most important pedagogy books in a generation. The case for play is stronger now than ever before and understanding its purpose is essential to any catch-up process after the Covid-19 interruptions. Play is the universal language of childhood and the richer the environment, the richer the opportunities are for self-expression, challenge and wellbeing amongst our youngest learners. How a child plays, or doesn't, tells us so much about their needs, their inner world and their state of mind. Sarah skilfully and organically uses the child's own voice to illustrate the most important factors in designing and using play environments for all educators to provide children with opportunities to develop language, resilience, relationships and wellbeing. This wonderful book should be a daily reference in all our learning settings.

Dr Sharie Coombes, author, ex-headteacher and neuropsychotherapist

I love this book on outdoor play, one of several in the Little Minds Matter series. It's an easy-to-read book for educators to read, reflect on and use to inspire their day-to-day outdoor practice with children. The photographs of Sarah's setting are truly remarkable and add an authentic feel to the book. I especially like the inclusion of children's voices; it's extremely important that we pay attention to children regarding their play and learning. Well done Sarah for writing this much-needed book for early years educators.

Laura Henry-Allain MBE, award-winning global writer, speaker, and consultant

There are people who contribute to the world of early years education without any actual experience within the setting. This book is the antidote to that tiresome commentary. Sarah Watkins has provided the hard-working and committed teacher with a fantastic guide to the awesome power of learning outside, building connections with nature, engaging in joint productive activities with children and the importance of relationships and wellbeing. This isn't just another teacher handbook, it's a handbook for the professional soul.

Hywel Roberts, author of Oops! Helping Children Learn Accidentally, *teacher, and storyteller*

It's not often that you come across a book that explores the importance of dragons, mud pies, puddles, magic and a laboratory of loose parts to the healthy development of children – this insightful book, richly embroidered with fascinating case studies and reflections is a must-buy for teachers, children's nurses, parents and anyone wanting to understand about the power of play in building resilience, confidence and a sense of belonging in our children.

Tony Warne, Chair of Stockport NHS Foundation Trust

I have been very fortunate during the last decade to work with and visit many different educational settings in the U.K. and internationally. Every time, without exception, I am blown away by the skill, expertise and proactive creative approaches that early years educators demonstrate every day. In this exciting new publication, Sarah harnesses her own considerable expertise along with the voices of young people themselves in a unique and exciting approach to the importance of play and well-being. Punctuated with reflection tasks and photos of children 'in action', this book really brings to life some of the magical learning I have been so fortunate to witness and continually learn. I imagine that this text will be invaluable to both new practitioners and also incredibly useful for experienced colleagues in equal measure, as Sarah draws the reader through a magical world with examples from across many different settings. Perhaps the highlight for me, the final word from Jack (which you will, of course, need to read for yourself…). This book is highly recommended and will, I am certain, prove to be a really invaluable addition to some of the most skilful educator's libraries and professional development materials around the world.

Gareth D. Morewood, Educational Advisor and previous
Secondary SENCo

As adults we must strive to nurture children's curiosity and playfulness and encourage independence. This book is a powerful reminder of our responsibility to take every opportunity to inspire children to learn more about the world in which they live, no matter their age. Highly recommended!

Nic Millington, CEO, Rural Media

This book is practical and accessible for primary practitioners to reflect on how they create the spaces, culture, and relationships for effective and authentic play. Each chapter is signposted by the values and the wellbeing themes it is exploring and encourages the reader to take time to reflect on their school's policy and practices, accompanied by signposting reading for both children and adults.

Hannah Wilson, Leadership Development Consultant, Coach,
and Trainer

Children need and love to play, explore and have adventures outside. This book embraces the benefits of exposing children to daring play and appropriate risk that is so helpful in addressing anxiety and fearful situations. It also highlights strategies to enable a healthy balance between safety and independence, as well as developing perseverance and resilience. This book provides the perfect framework to create a culture of care and wellbeing through play at school.

Patrick Ottley-O'Connor, Executive Headteacher

This book helps adults understand how they can create environments and resources for children to explore play through relationships and curiosity. It also makes some important points on playing alongside children and how fundamental play is for all families and communities. An interesting read with many good ideas.

Mike Armiger, education and mental health advisor

There has never been a more important time to foster the wellbeing of children and Sarah's fantastic book shows you how to do that through the important business of play. I love the mix of theory, research and practical ideas, all brought to life with the voices and perspectives of children. Sarah is an experienced teacher and her wisdom shines through each page – this is a must read for any early years practitioner and primary school teacher.

Adrian Bethune, Teachappy

Access your online resources

Outdoor Play for Healthy Little Minds is accompanied by a number of printable online materials, designed to ensure this resource best supports your professional needs.

Download your online resources:
Go to www.routledge.com/9780367683436 and click Support Material.

Outdoor Play for Healthy Little Minds

This essential resource is designed to help busy early years practitioners to support the mental health of young children through outdoor play.

Promoting social and emotional wellbeing in childhood has never been more important, and outdoor play is a crucial tool to build resilience, develop healthy relationships, and boost self-esteem. Using relatable case studies that demonstrate achievable change, this book is full of practical advice and strategies for exploring nature in both natural and man-made landscapes, and includes guidance on how to co-create inviting play spheres with children.

Each chapter provides:

- Adaptable and cost-effective activities designed to help children feel more confident and connected to the world around them.
- Case studies and reflective opportunities to prompt practitioners to consider and develop their own practice.
- An accessible and engaging format with links to theorists, risk assessment, and individual schemas.

Outdoor play allows young children to explore who they are and what they can do. It supports them as they learn to think critically, take risks, and form a true sense of belonging with their peers and with the wider community. This is an indispensable resource for practising and trainee early years practitioners, Reception teachers, and childminders as they facilitate outdoor play in their early years setting.

Sarah Watkins is a Reception teacher and Forest School leader who is passionate about the positive impact of outdoor play on children's wellbeing. Sarah's memories of an outdoor, play-filled childhood inform her teaching ethos, and, as Head of School, Sarah knew the location of all the best hiding places, as it was the primary school she attended as a child! Before teaching, Sarah worked as an Arts Officer, and also managed projects for a national media charity, giving a platform to unheard voices. Sarah is a Specialist Leader in Education and university tutor who regularly speaks at educational events.

Little Minds Matter:

Promoting Social and Emotional Wellbeing in the Early Years

Series Advisor: Sonia Mainstone-Cotton

The *Little Minds Matter* series promotes best practice for integrating social and emotional health and wellbeing into the early years setting. It introduces practitioners to a wealth of activities and resources to support them in each key area: from providing access to ideas for unstructured, imaginative outdoor play; activities to create a sense of belonging and form positive identities; and, importantly, strategies to encourage early years professionals to create a workplace that positively contributes to their own wellbeing, as well as the quality of their provision. The *Little Minds Matter* series ensures that practitioners have the tools they need to support every child.

Outdoor Play for Healthy Little Minds
Practical Ideas to Promote Children's Wellbeing in the Early Years
Sarah Watkins

Supporting the Wellbeing of Children with SEND
Essential Ideas for Early Years Educators
Kerry Payne

Outdoor Play for Healthy Little Minds

Practical Ideas to Promote Children's Wellbeing in the Early Years

Sarah Watkins

Routledge
Taylor & Francis Group

LONDON AND NEW YORK

First published 2022
by Routledge
2 Park Square, Milton Park, Abingdon, Oxon OX14 4RN

and by Routledge
605 Third Avenue, New York, NY 10158

Routledge is an imprint of the Taylor & Francis Group, an informa business

British Library Cataloguing-in-Publication Data
A catalogue record for this book is available from the British Library

Library of Congress Cataloging-in-Publication Data
Names: Watkins, Sarah, 1972- author.
Title: Outdoor play for healthy little minds : practical ideas to promote children's wellbeing in the early years / Sarah Watkins.
Description: Abingdon, Oxon ; New York, NY : Routledge, 2022. |
Series: Little minds matter | Includes bibliographical references and index.
Identifiers: LCCN 2021020519 (print) | LCCN 2021020520 (ebook) |
ISBN 9780367683443 (hardback) | ISBN 9780367683436 (paperback) |
ISBN 9781003137023 (ebook)
Subjects: LCSH: Play. | Early childhood education--Activity programs. |
Outdoor education. | Nature study. | Child mental health.
Classification: LCC LB1139.35.P55 W384 2022 (print) | LCC LB1139.35.P55 (ebook) |
DDC 372.13--dc23
LC record available at https://lccn.loc.gov/2021020519
LC ebook record available at https://lccn.loc.gov/2021020520

ISBN: 978-0-367-68344-3 (hbk)
ISBN: 978-0-367-68343-6 (pbk)
ISBN: 978-1-003-13702-3 (ebk)

DOI: 10.4324/9781003137023

Typeset in Optima
by Deanta Global Publishing Services, Chennai, India

Photographs by Sarah Watkins and friends.

Access the Support Material: www.routledge.com/9780367683436

Contents

Acknowledgements

Above all I want to thank my current and previous pupils. You've shown me the power of play. A huge thanks to Ledbury Primary School and Headteacher, Julie Rees, for supporting me on this journey.

Thank you to every child and adult whose voice is within this book.

Thank you to the endlessly patient and wise Clare Ashworth and Leah Burton at Speechmark. Debbie Garvey, thank you for setting me on this path, and for your continued friendship and wisdom. Dr Sharie Coombes, you shared with me experiences that changed your life and, in doing so, you changed my life too. Thank you to Adrian Bethune, Greg Bottrill, Ben Tawil, Tim Gill, Jan White, Suzanne Axelsson, Lisa Atkinson, Julie Jones, and Ann Gladstone for your invaluable help. Thank you to Janine Medway-Smith, an exceptional teacher and leader. Bridget Knight, thank you for your guidance and your kindness. Georgina Young, thank you for your continual support. Thank you to Carly for lending me your beautiful children. Thank you to Zayla Beecham for taking the photographs on pages 23, 24, 32, 64 and 125. Thank you to Toni Cook for coffees and support!

A huge thank you to the following people for providing me with feedback: Kate Barker, Andy and Hazel Dowling, Ian Broady, Rachael Roper, Catherine Adkins, Phoebe Ayling, Frances Tait, Lauren Craig, Thea Preece, Jo Gilks, Sarah Sheppard.

To my parents, Abby and Bill Laws, thank you for giving me a play-filled childhood. To my sisters, Kahlia and Rosie, thank you for being my play companions.

This book would never have been written without my husband, Rob, who always has faith in me.

Thank you to my children, Ethan and Theodore who took me on an unforgettable outdoor play journey.

Foreword

It feels exciting to be launching the new series of Little Minds Matter with this first book on outdoor play by Sarah Watkins. Our hope for this series is to pull together many different voices from across the early years field, sharing their ideas, passions, expertise, and insights into how we support children's wellbeing. We all know that if we can get this right in the early years, it sets a firm and solid foundation for children's ongoing mental health.

Spending time outdoors is crucial for children's wellbeing; there is increasing evidence and research to back this. We have seen and experienced, during the last year with COVID, how important the outdoors and engaging in nature is for all of us. It feels so timely to be launching this series with Sarah's book. Sarah explores why the outdoors is so crucial for children's wellbeing and shares ideas on how we can help children to spend more time outside. As I read this book, I found myself smiling and expressing joy as I saw her many wonderful ideas and suggestions around outdoor play, exploration, and how essential these are to children's wellbeing. Sarah shares her own experiences and learning of discovering the outdoors for herself and with the children she has worked alongside. I was particularly thrilled to read about her foraging with children!

Throughout this book, Sarah has woven in children's voices; this brings a depth and insight to the reader that can sometimes be overlooked. Sarah shares practical and varied resources and ideas, both from her own experience and through the case examples of others from across the world. Children's rights and ownership form an integral part of her work; she offers many inspiring examples of how children have ownership in the outdoor spaces they use and the learning and development that come from this.

Outdoor play and exploration as a tool to boost children's and adults' wellbeing have been an integral part of my work and writing, and it is always a joy to read this in others' work. After reading this book, I felt an increased motivation to get outside, increase my discovery of the outdoors around me, and continue having this foundation of my work with children.

I am sure you will enjoy this book. I hope you are inspired to get outside and plant a seed, look for bugs, or climb a tree, either on your own or with the children you work alongside. I hope this book brings you the delight it brought me.

Sonia Mainstone-Cotton
Series Advisor
April 2021

Introduction

"When I am outside, playing, I run so fast with Robert, then we lied down on the grass, and he was laughing and laughing on my tummy!" Julie

The first day

Levi crawled inside the den he'd made and chattered happily to two friends. He used his binoculars to spy through a gap in the material at a group of children digging in the sand. Levi was proud of his complex 'doorbell' system, rigged up using a piece of rope, but he shrieked in happiness when a friend ignored this and burst noisily into the den.

In the classroom though, Levi was silent and withdrawn. This was Levi's first day in my first ever class. He lingered watchfully at the edges of the classroom, occasionally running his fingers over objects. When I called the register, Levi stood, hunched, by the door. He eyed his peers suspiciously. After the register, I invited Levi to come and sit with me on the floor so that we could share a book. As we looked at the pages together, Levi suddenly said: "I was rubbish at my other school." What had made a four-year-old feel this way? In that moment, I felt determined to help Levi see himself as a capable and valued member of our class.

DOI: 10.4324/9781003137023-101

Making space

Unfortunately, Levi's case is not an isolated one. Dr Sharie Coombes, a neuropsychotherapist and author, uses her self-devised Creative Play Technique to treat children:

> Although they cannot articulate it, you can see it in their behaviour, and in the way they present themselves: many of today's children feel inadequate, and they feel there's no space for them. There's so much focus on getting it right and doing things the right way. They don't ever learn their own capacity.

Levi recognised that adults were trying to fix his 'deficiencies' and developed an overwhelming sense of incompetence. Left unchecked, this can cause long-lasting adverse effects. "It frames who you become, what you believe about yourself and how you limit yourself," comments Dr Coombes.

Playing outside, Levi felt more self-assured and was motivated to try and sometimes fail, perhaps because there was less adult surveillance. "Play," says Dr Coombes, "offers children a way to shape their sense of capacity, their sense of competence, their sense of connection, their sense of creativity." Although adult-directed learning offers important opportunities to teach skills and build relationships, we need to ensure balance.

In this book, you'll find research on child-led outdoor play and wellbeing, as well as tried and tested ideas and strategies. In addition, each chapter includes a case study featuring a practitioner with expertise in the field of outdoor play. Children from across the UK were also interviewed for this book. I hope you enjoy their refreshingly honest insights.

Wellbeing: feeling good and doing well

"When we go in forest school, I go by the dragon and in the hiding place, and my tummy and all of me feels like the sunshine." Imogen

'Wellbeing' is a problematic term to define, and it's open to many different interpretations. When I discussed it with colleagues, they used phrases like 'cared for' and 'thriving'. The four-year-olds in my class had never come across the word 'wellbeing,' but when asked about happiness, they mentioned smiling and laughing, and almost every child  talked about play. One child commented: "all the people should play to be happy!"

Adrian Bethune, author of *Wellbeing in the Primary Classroom*, offers the following definition of wellbeing: "living a life where one regularly experiences positive emotions (like joy, peace, love, curiosity, fun), feels like overall life is going well, together with feeling engaged in work and interests, and having a sense of meaning and purpose" (Bethune, 2018). A child's sense of purpose should be rooted in what is important to them, and outdoor play gives children the opportunity to set themselves meaningful challenges that excite and intrigue them.

I often use the definition 'feeling good and doing well', and Dr Michelle McQuaid, playful change activator, and author of a book with this title, talks about the importance of resilience. Resilience enables us to cope with the inevitable difficulties we encounter in life without becoming overwhelmed.

So how do children develop resilience? Dr Ann Masten, whose research focuses on factors that enhance resilience, proposes that it emerges through 'ordinary magic': interactions with the environment and relationships with competent, caring adults. (Masten, 2015) Part of our role then, as practitioners, is enabling access to environmental experiences, and building competence and strengths. (Masten, 2015)

For Levi, feeling good and doing well relied on his believing that he was a competent individual and that adults believed this too. Competence, along with autonomy and relatedness, is a psychological need that humans must fulfil in order to function well according to self-determination theory (SDT). Just remember the acronym, CAR:

3

- **C**ompetence: mastering different skills in order to feel ready and motivated to attempt challenging goals. (Appropriate feedback helps us feel more competent.)
- **A**utonomy: feeling in control of our own behaviours and goals and believing that we can effect change. (We feel less in control if our behaviours are mainly controlled by extrinsic rewards.)
- **R**elatedness: we need to feel a sense of belonging and attachment to other people. Our relationships and interactions are crucial (Ryan and Deci, 2017). I would add that we also need to feel a sense of belonging to the natural world as this can restore us.

For good emotional wellbeing, children need to have some control over what they do and how they do it, whilst also enjoying strong, healthy relationships. In this book, we'll explore ways that outdoor play can help children become capable, independent, and connected individuals.

 TIME TO REFLECT:

Take a moment to think about the 'ordinary magic' that goes on at your setting. (Remember, you are key to this magic!)

The Leuven Scales of wellbeing and involvement

"Wellbeing is the beautiful stage in which children can be when they feel OK. They feel at ease. They radiate. They are open to anything that comes in." Ferre Laevers

So how do we establish a child's level of wellbeing? It's down to that third fundamental of CAR: relatedness. We know and understand the children in our settings, and we work closely with parents and carers, taking a holistic approach. We quickly pick up on cues that tell us if a child is worried, stressed, anxious, or unhappy. We recognise that transitions can affect a child's emotional wellbeing.

Alongside this, a wellbeing assessment tool such as the Leuven Scales, if used correctly, can show patterns and preferences, helping us see how well the environment is working to support wellbeing. The Leuven Scales were developed by the Research Centre for Experiential Education (RCEE) at Leuven University, under the supervision of Dr Ferre Laevers. There are indicators to look for in children's play, and the evaluation process begins by observing pupils as a group or individually for approximately two minutes. Low levels could indicate that the environment needs adapting, although it's important to remember that wellbeing is dynamic and it's natural for levels to fluctuate throughout the day.

According to Dr Laevers, if children have a high level of wellbeing and high engagement in their environment, they feel comfortable in their surroundings and can fully be themselves. We've all seen children enjoying that immersive play stage that Laevers describes as being "a fish in water."

Tables 0.1 and 0.2 show the Leuven Scales for wellbeing and involvement, but remember that these scales are not designed to be used as a 'tick

Table 0.1 The Leuven Scale for wellbeing

Level	Wellbeing	Signals
1	Extremely low	The child shows clear signs of distress, such as crying or screaming. They may look dejected, sad, frightened, or angry. The child does not respond to the environment, avoids contact, and is withdrawn. The child may behave aggressively, hurting him/herself or others.
2	Low	The posture, facial expression, and actions indicate that the child does not feel at ease. However, the signals are less explicit than level 1, or the sense of discomfort is not expressed the whole time.
3	Moderate	The child has a neutral posture. Facial expression and posture show little or no emotion. There are no signs indicating sadness or pleasure, comfort or discomfort.
4	High	The child shows obvious signs of satisfaction (as listed under level 5). However, these signals are not constantly present with the same intensity.
5	Extremely high	The child looks happy and cheerful, smiles, cries out with pleasure. They may be lively and full of energy. Actions can be spontaneous and expressive. The child may talk to him/herself, play with sounds, hum, sing. The child appears relaxed and does not show any signs of stress or tension. He/she is open and accessible to the environment. The child expresses self-confidence and self-assurance.

Table 0.2 The Leuven Scale of involvement

Level	Wellbeing	Signals
1	Extremely low	Activity is simple, repetitive, and passive. The child seems absent and displays no energy. They may stare into space or look around to see what others are doing.
2	Low	Frequently interrupted activity. The child will be engaged in the activity for some of the time they are observed, but there will be moments of non-activity when they will stare into space or be distracted by what is going on around them.
3	Moderate	Mainly continuous activity. The child is busy with the activity, but at a reasonably routine level, and there are few signs of real involvement. They make some progress with what they are doing, but don't show much energy and concentration and can be easily distracted.
4	High	Continuous activity with intense moments. The child's activity has intense moments, and at times they seem involved. They are not easily distracted.
5	Extremely high	The child shows continuous and intense activity revealing the greatest involvement. They are concentrated, creative, energetic, and persistent throughout nearly all the observed period.

list' to assess children's wellbeing, but rather to determine how well the environment meets the needs of the children using it.

TIME TO REFLECT:

A child has been standing by the sand for ten minutes. He lifts sand up and lets it fall through his fingers over and over again. He shows signs of level 3 involvement. Would you change the environment? What else would inform your judgement?

Action points

The RCEE has produced a list of ten action points to consider after using the scales, and these points could easily be applied to an outdoor space:

1. Rearrange the classroom in appealing corners or areas.
2. Check the content of the areas and make them more challenging.
3. Introduce new and unconventional materials and activities.
4. Identify children's interests and offer activities that meet these.
5. Support activities by stimulating inputs.
6. Widen the possibilities for free initiative and support them with sound agreements.
7. Improve the quality of the relations amongst children and between children and teacher(s).
8. Introduce activities that help children explore the world of behaviour, feelings, and values.
9. Identify children with emotional problems and work out sustaining interventions.
10. Identify children with developmental needs and work out interventions that engender involvement.

(Laevers, 2006)

Discussing our observations and interpretations as a staff team can generate unexpected insights, as well as addressing the issue of unconscious bias. Of course, we are the vital component, and Laevers points out that our interactions with children are key to wellbeing and involvement.

What is play?

"*Playing is when* <u>*we*</u> *choose, not the teacher.*" Jack

Most of us would confidently state that we could recognise play when we see it. However, what constitutes play can be subjective. For example, each setting tends to have rules around what is allowed in play, and sometimes this can define 'play' versus 'not play'. Once, while employed as an Arts Officer, I organised a sculpture project for young children at a pupil referral unit. We were working on individual sculptures outside, and a teacher told one child that, since he had finished his artwork, he could "go and play." The child promptly scaled the fence and ran away across a field. "That's not play!" shouted the teacher. "Yes, it bloody is!" yelled back the jubilant child.

When I asked the children in my class: "what is play?" many used words linked to choice and "not work." All became enthusiastic when discussing play and began describing specific examples of their favourite ways to play – they found it easier to discuss *how* they play.

Psychologist Dr Peter Gray proposes that play is self-chosen, self-directed, and intrinsically motivated (Gray, 2013). Children often simply want to get on with the 'work of play' but this doesn't mean adults are redundant. Far from it. Adults tend to design and resource the outdoor environment, and young children often want adults to be attentive and engaged.

Watching some of my pupils outdoors yesterday, I was struck by how different play behaviours can be. I saw three children conferring quietly in a den; six children being superheroes, running and chasing; eight children using loose parts to make a 'bonfire'; two children being horses; three children riding bikes down a grassed slope; and one child moving worms from a puddle to the grass, using a twig. Play is as varied as the children themselves.

What does play look like?

Bob Hughes, a play theorist and activist, has identified 16 types of play, described in more detail in his book: *A Playworker's Taxonomy of Play Types* (Hughes and Melville, 2002). Table 0.3 provides a short description of Bob's play types. Just remember that there will often be overlap between the different types.

Using this list can help us see which types of play are most prevalent in the outdoor environment, and whether this space allows for *all* types of play – for example, do children have access to quiet spaces for communication play? Discussion with colleagues about how they would classify observed play behaviours

can be insightful: we see these things differently sometimes!

TIME TO REFLECT:

Young children are skilled users of technology. Digital play is another category that could be added to the list above. How do you feel about this?

Table 0.3 Types of play by Bob Hughes

Type of play	Description	Example
Symbolic play	Children use objects, actions, or ideas to represent other objects, actions, or ideas as play. Control and exploration in a safe space.	Using stones and pebbles as tea and cakes.
Rough-and-tumble play	Close encounter play which is less to do with fighting and more to do with touching, tickling, and gauging relative strength. Discovering physical flexibility and the exhilaration of display.	Superhero play where 'goodies' and 'baddies' do battle.
Socio-dramatic play	Children act out real and potential experiences.	Playing house.
Social play	Any social or interactive situation where the expectation is that everyone will follow the set rules.	Playing tag.
Creative play	Children explore, try out ideas, and use their imagination. Altering something or making something new.	Creating something using loose parts.
Communication play	Play using words, nuances, or gestures.	Charades, mime, telling jokes, play-acting.
Dramatic play	Play which dramatises events in which the child is not a direct participant.	Dressing up.
Deep play	Play that allows children to encounter risky experiences, develop survival skills, and conquer fear.	Tree climbing.
Exploratory play	Using senses of smell, touch, and even taste to explore and discover the texture and function of things around them.	Swinging on a rope swing.
Fantasy play	Play which rearranges the world in the child's way. They get to play things out that are unlikely to occur.	Pretending to be astronauts.
Imaginative play	Play where the conventional rules, which govern the physical world, do not apply.	Pretending to be cats.
Locomotor play	Movement in any or every direction for its own sake because it's fun.	Running or chasing
Mastery play	Control of the physical and affective ingredients of the environment.	Digging a hole in the sand to fill with water.
Object play	Play that uses infinite and interesting sequences of hand-eye manipulations and movements.	Rolling conkers through a tube.

(Continued)

Table 0.3 (Continued) Types of play by Bob Hughes

Type of play	Description	Example
Role play	Play exploring ways of being, although not generally of an intense personal, social, domestic, or interpersonal nature.	Being a strict teacher.
Recapitulative play	Allows the child to explore ancestry, history, rituals, stories, rhymes, fire, and darkness. Enables children to access play of earlier human evolutionary stages. Recapitulative play is the most controversial of the 16 categories, and there is some debate about whether it exists.	Examples would include building shelters or making weapons.

Historical theories of outdoor play

In the early 18th century, people saw childhood as a highly dangerous period to be hurried through – two-thirds of children died before they reached the age of five. Towards the end of the 18th century, child mortality rates fell dramatically and suddenly childhood became associated with freedom, creativity, emotion, and malleability (Reynolds, 2014). People began to think differently about play and children's capacities.

One of these people was Friedrich Froebel, who opened the first kindergarten or 'garden of children' in 1826. Froebel recognised that children's brains develop significantly during the first three years of life, and he believed that learning was driven by play. Froebel's kindergarten included gardening spaces, animals to care for, nature walk routes, and loose natural play materials for exploration. Froebel strongly believed that play should be nurtured through adult guidance and he felt play influenced a child's development as a whole.

Dr Maria Montessori, one of Italy's first female doctors, felt that every child should be immersed in nature, and encouraged children to take ownership of their own learning. Dr Montessori's Casa dei Bambini opened in 1906 in a deprived inner-city district of Rome. She advocated "bringing the inside out and the outside in," and every Montessori school had a plot of land that the children were responsible for.

The McMillan sisters, Rachel and Margaret, also believed in giving children responsibility, and encouraged children to look after plants and animals in order to learn about the importance of caring for themselves and others.

The McMillan Open Air Nursery School, thought to be the first in England, opened in 1914, and there was a strong emphasis on children being self-reliant. The McMillans prioritised learning outdoors and child-led play, at a time when playing outside was generally seen as a break from indoor academic activities. The McMillans believed strongly that children learn through exploration.

At the start of this section, we looked at the way that childhood was seen as a dangerous period to be hurried through. In 1981, Dr David Elkind proposed that children were once again being 'hurried through' childhood, this time by busy, stressed adults who were pushing children to grow up too fast, missing out on vital, active, exploratory play (Elkind, 1981).

TIME TO REFLECT:

How have these educational theorists influenced outdoor play provision today?

The decline of outdoor play

"There's grass near our flat, but we only go there with mummy, not on our own. We don't go there if it is raining." Luis

Today's children spend much less time playing outdoors than their counterparts did 50 years ago. A 2016 study found that more than one in nine children in England had not set foot in a park, forest, beach, or any other natural environment for at least 12 months (Hunt et al., 2016).

One reason may be that outdoor play can arouse suspicion and concern amongst the general public. Psychotherapist Dr Dorothy Judd took her five-year-old grandson, Max, into the local woods to play. They built a den, collecting branches and sticks and using a flat stone as a doormat. Max pretended to cook dinner. Dr Judd comments:

I joined in, pleased he was so happy and imaginative … pleased that he didn't mind slugs, worms or mud on his hands. Seeing his small frame ahead of me, nimbly stepping over branches, roots and stones like a woodland elf, I knew that this was another blessed moment in my store of beautiful times granted by our grandchildren.

The next day, Max wanted to carry on with his den play, and they returned to the same part of the woods. However, a police officer suddenly appeared and escorted them out of the woods because members of the public had complained about their 'suspicious behaviour'. "I half wonder," comments Dr Judd, "if I had been stupid to play in this way, to allow Max to create this imaginary world in a wood."

Months later, Max wanted to return to the woods with Dr Judd and her husband. Max led them back to the den, which had miraculously survived the winter. Although Max pointed out some of the details such as the fireplace and the doormat, he no longer wanted to play in the den. Dr Judd comments: "While I felt safe this time, there was little magic for me. Max and I did not enter into that fantasy world again" (Judd, 2008).

Unfortunately, this is not the only case of police being called to investigate outdoor play in recent years, and a culture of surveillance seems to have developed.

TIME TO REFLECT:

How does this example make you feel?

All to play for

"The opposite of play is depression." Brian Sutton Smith (Sutton-Smith, 2001)

Outdoor play in the community is in decline and, at the same time, mental health issues are rising rapidly. According to reports, children's happiness declines year on year (Good Childhood Report, 2020) and one in six school-aged children has a mental health issue (NHS Digital, 2020). More children than ever are struggling to cope. On average, there is a ten-year delay between children displaying symptoms and getting help (Centre for Mental Health, 2019).

The skills that children need to cope with and navigate difficult situations are social and emotional skills (Anna Freud Centre, n.d.) and these include:

- Being self-aware
- Managing feelings and behaviour
- Social awareness
- Building and managing healthy relationships
- Making good decisions
    (Collaborative for Academic, Social, and Emotional Learning, 2019)

In the next section, you'll find observations of outdoor play at settings in Scotland, Thailand, Wales, France, England, and the Netherlands. As you read through, think about the social and emotional learning that is evident in each observation.

Children at play

The Netherlands

Failure doesn't come easily to him. Indoors he is the smartest and quickest thinker; there is nothing he can't do ... indoors. He has a debilitating condition that makes large movement difficult. Outdoors is his nemesis; outdoors, he is not king of the castle, and it bothers him. Every morning he is the first to access the outdoor provision. He sits and slowly puts on his rain trousers and boots. It's an enormous task, but he doesn't give up. His friends are off running long before his trouser elastic is secured under his boot. Every day I watch, silently telling myself to hold back, wait, and let him do it by himself. He's up and off, his stiff-legged gait propelling him forward. He falls; he uses his upper body strength to get himself back up to standing. With a quick look back, he gives me a thumbs up and a nod to say: "I'm OK, I've got this." I watch from a distance as he joins his friends in a game of football. The transition into the game is smooth, and I hear him narrate what he is doing for his friends "I'm going to run this way so that I can get the ball, watch me kick it, I can kick it so hard! I got the ball, run, run, run, I can do this!" With unbending knees, the ball goes far wide of the designated goal. It doesn't deter him; "Did you see that? I nearly got a goal that time; I am getting so good at football. My dad is going to take me to a team so that I can play outside of school too, did you know that?" I continue watching as his friends rally around him, congratulating him on great passes. The game continues long after he has passed the limit of his pain threshold. He doesn't stop. The winces become more pronounced, and the falls more frequent. He plays on.

Jennifer ten Wolde, reception teacher, the Netherlands

Thailand

The new girl is tentative in the water area. This is a hot and humid climate, so there is often a culture of not doing much outside if it can be helped. Most children at this school come from upper-middle-class families where there is often stigma attached to tanned skin, and so they have often spent most of their early years in air-conditioned places.

But she can see that the other two girls are having a great time scooping, pouring, and pushing the plastic balls around in the pool. She shuffles over to the guttering and starts pouring water down the chute using a watering can, gazing at the other two all the while.

She laughs when the two girls climb into the pool, sit in the water, and start tossing balls to one another, giggling. She goes over to them, still laughing. She stands at the side, watching and chatting a little in Thai. It might be a few weeks before she's getting in as well, but already she doesn't mind getting splashed.

James Haddell, nursery setting, Thailand

France

Every week we go to the forest across the road from our school. M is five years old and already speaks three languages. Exuberant and full of curiosity, M's play is usually physical, constantly testing the laws of physics (throwing, bouncing, spinning, pressing, squirting, etc.). On this occasion, we have taken some containers along to Forest School with us, and M starts making different shakers. Quietly and on his own, he tests the sounds, adding first acorns, then pebbles, leaves, and small pieces of broken twig. Each time, he adds a collection of loose parts, shakes, listens, then empties out the bottle and repeats with another collection. He sees me watching and includes me, asking me to listen to each shaker after he has tested it. I take some photos, and we post them together online. We talked about other ways we could use objects in the forest to play with making sound. Over at least three forest sessions, M explored sound in the forest. It became his 'thing', his research. The post online allowed his parents to discuss the sound enquiry with him. He opened up his enquiry to other children when they approached him, and some stayed for a while, but M's stamina outlasted his peers' interest. Over the course of the sessions, he shared his findings with me – the snapping of leaves, drumming on trees, clashes of stones, etc. In the forest, he was an instrument maker, a composer, and a musician, and he was proud to have these titles. Back in class and at home, his explorations continued using instruments, loose parts, and Chrome Music Lab.

Estelle Ash, the International School of Toulouse, France

London, England

I stand watching a girl stirring the mud in her frying pan. She chats to herself: "need some chocolate sauce, mud sprinkles, this is it." Some boys join her: "I got some more water guys; we are making soup for everyone." Her chocolate sauce becomes soup for everyone. She talks to the group, not to anyone in particular: "Please, can I just do it for a minute, only one scoop. Right you guys, stay here mixing while I get another bit." She asks herself where one of the boys has gone. The frying pan falls to the floor. She says: "Oh we need to pick it all up now, our potion has breaked. Can you help me because this is a risaster?" We scoop it up together, in silence. The boys have disappeared, and she finds a ball of sticky tape, which she adds to the pan and begins to stir. She begins to quietly chat to herself.

> My mummy, like my mummy's mum, she just be dead. And then she went up into the sky. Am I gonna be dead? I'm not gonna be dead, or my mummy or my daddy, 'cause I want them to look after me, so when I'm old, when they're just like old, they will be dead, and they will fly in the sky. And then just me

and Levi. Just me and Levi, not someone else looking after me. This is good. Where's Josh gone? I'm gonna find Josh.

I'm glad I stood back and observed and let her thoughts play out, let her speak them as she tried to make sense of things. She never once looked at me while she was talking.

Janine Medway-Smith, Hampden Way Nursery, London

Wales

My school invested in a wood-based outdoor trail, obstacle course. It consisted of balance bars, a climbing wall, balance stumps, a rope balance, monkey bars, and an 'A-frame' rope climbing frame. One child was too scared to climb the 'A-frame'. "I've never been that high before." For many days I observed him trying to climb up the first few steps, then giving up. Any adult offers of help were dismissed. A few weeks later, we visited our local woodland gardens where there is a large, felled tree labelled as 'nature's climbing frame'. It goes up quite high and has an element of risk due to the slippery surface of the bark in places and the differences in width of the trunk. This particular child didn't hesitate when given the go ahead to climb the tree, albeit slowly. He did it many times without fear. I couldn't believe how confident he was. He was so pleased with himself! When we got back to school, once again, this child was too afraid to climb the climbing frame despite having navigated the felled tree with ease. When I asked him why, he replied: "I will fall … I don't feel safe." However, after a few days, he conquered his fear and climbed over the top and down the other side. I have always thought about the reasons why this child felt more comfortable in the woodland than he did in school. I think he needed a different environment to improve his physical development skills, and then our outdoor school environment was able to complement them.

Cara Edwards, Templeton CP School, Wales

Scotland

One afternoon during free flow play, I noticed an uncommonly long lull in the sounds of noisy play that usually ring out across our outdoors provision.

There were no children running, screaming, jumping, laughing, dancing, playing football, singing, building … instead, the ten children who had chosen to play outside were all gathered around a bench, whispering to each other. In the midst of their huddle was a tiny garden snail. I stood back to observe. It was clear that one child was leading the group: "No, guys, don't scream! He might be scared!" She started assigning each of the children different tasks, offering feedback and adding more instructions as each 'job' progressed: "He might be lonely. He needs some friends. You look in the hedge." A few children used plastic tennis rackets to carry back more snails. "Well done. Look at these two tiny ones that are so cute and tiny. They're babies." "They need loads of grass to eat, and they might have a snooze over here. You get grass." One child brought a small handful of grass back to the bench. "For them to eat! They've eaten quite a lot. You need to get more." "They need somewhere to live, so they don't get cold. This is their home under here." She pointed to the outdoor resources trolley as the snails' new home: the group whispered agreement. "You take the food. I'll take these guys back to the house where they are safe." Tongue poking out in concentration, she carefully carried the snails to the trolley (egg-and-spoon-race-style, using the plastic tennis racket) and placed them on the ground underneath. The group all huddled around the trolley, watching the snails move around their new home. For the entire day, the same children spent every minute of their free play caring for the snails. I was invited to visit and was asked, at different points, to provide resources: a bowl for water, bricks to build a wall for shelter, recycling materials to make furniture…

Following on from this play observation, we introduced a class minibeasts topic to learn all about snails and their "creepy-crawly friends from the garden."

Charlotte Bowes, St. Joseph's RC Primary School, Scotland

Conclusion

In these international examples of outdoor play, we can clearly see children developing competence, autonomy, and relatedness. These children are working out who they are and what they can do, they are determined and tenacious, they are processing emotions and thinking critically. In each instance, the adult is present, attentive, supportive, and interested, and this 'strengths' educational model contrasts sharply with the 'deficit' model of education that Levi endured.

I qualified as a teacher just over a decade ago. Levi is now a much more self-confident teenager, although he still struggles sometimes with an education system that prioritises academic achievement over emotional wellbeing. When he leaves school, Levi's goal is to become a tree surgeon, and I like to think this is down to his tree climbing days when I was his teacher!

TIME TO REFLECT:

- What are your memories of outdoor play?
- What do you feel could be done at a government level to improve children's wellbeing?
- How do you define wellbeing? Is there a clear definition used by your setting that all staff understand?
- Using the Leuven Scales, can you identify any changes that could be made to your outdoor play environment?
- When you observe outdoor play in your setting, are there any of the 16 types of play behaviour that you see less often? How could you change the resourcing in response to this?

References

Reading for children

Coombes, S., Larmour, C., Willow, M. and Catt, H. (2020). *A Dragon Called Worry*. Sywell: Autumn Publishing.

Singer, M. and Pham, L. (2012). *A Stick Is an Excellent Thing: Poems Celebrating Outdoor Play*. Boston: Clarion Books.

Witek, J. and Roussey, C. (2015). *In My Heart: A Book of Feelings*. New York: Abrams Appleseed.

Reading for adults

Anna Freud Centre. (n.d.). *Social and Emotional Skills*. Mentally Healthy Schools. [online] www.mentallyhealthyschools.org.uk. Available at: https://www.mentallyhealthyschools.org.uk/getting-started/social-and-emotional-skills/.

Axline, V. (2009). *Dibs: In Search of Self.* Brantford: W. Ross Macdonald School Resource Services Library.

Bethune, A. (2018). *Wellbeing in the Primary Classroom: A Practical Guide to Teaching Happiness*. London: Bloomsbury.

Bottrill, G. (2018). *Can I Go and Play Now? Rethinking Continuous Provision for the Early Years*. London: Sage.

Centre for Mental Health. (2019). *Fact Sheet: Children and Young People's Mental Health*. Centre for Mental Health. [online] Cen treformentalhealth.org.uk. Available at: https://www.centreforment alhealth.org.uk/fact-sheet-children-and-young-peoples-mental -health.

Cohen, D. (2019). *The Development of Play*. New York: Routledge.

Collaborative for Academic, Social, and Emotional Learning. (2019). *What Is SEL?* [online] Casel.org. Available at: https://casel.org/what -is-sel/.

Elkind, D. (1981). *Hurried Child: Growing Up Too Fast Too Soon*. Reading: Addison-Wesley.

Ephgrave, A. (2015). *Reception Year in Action: A Month-by-Month Guide to Success in the Classroom*. Routledge.

Garner, S. (2020). *Mental Health in Education: Building Good Foundations*. New York: Routledge.

Gray, P. (2013). *Free to Learn: Why Unleashing the Instinct to Play Will Make Our Children Happier, More Self-Reliant, and Better Prepared for Life*. New York: Basic Books.

Hughes, B. and Melville, S. (2002). *A Playworkers' Taxonomy of Play Types*. London: Playlink.

Hunt, A., Stewart, D., Burt, J. and Dillon, J. (2016). *Monitor of Engagement with the Natural Environment: A Pilot to Develop an*

Indicator of Visits to the Natural Environment by Children - Results from Years 1 and 2 (March 2013 to February 2015). Natural England Commissioned Reports, 208.

Judd, D. (2008). Did they think I had kidnapped him? *The Guardian.* Available at: https://www.theguardian.com/uk/2008/jul/21/familya ndrelationships [Accessed 30 December 2020].

Laevers, F. (2005). *Well-Being and Involvement in Care Settings. A Process-Oriented Self-Evaluation Instrument.* (Ed. Ferre Laevers). Research Centre for Experiential Education, Leuven: Leuven University.

Laevers, F. (2006). *Making Care and Education More Effective through Wellbeing and Involvement. An Introduction to Experiential Education.* Research Centre for Experiential Education, University of Leuven, Belgium.

Masten, A.S. (2015). *Ordinary Magic: Resilience in Development.* New York: The Guilford Press.

Mcquaid, M. and Kern, P. (2018). *Your Wellbeing Blueprint: Feeling Good and Doing Well At Work.* Victoria: Michelle Mcquaid.

Moore, L., Turner, A. and Crellin, R. (2020). *The Good Childhood Report.* London: The Children's Society. doi:10.13140/RG.2.2.28456.80643

NHS Digital. (2020). *Mental Health of Children and Young People in England, 2020: Wave 1 Follow Up to the 2017 Survey.* [online]. Available at: https://digital.nhs.uk/data-andinformation/publications /statistical/mental-health-of-children-and-young-people-in-england /2020-wave-1-follow-up [Accessed 1 February 2021].

Reynolds, K. (2014). *Perceptions of Childhood.* [online] The British Library. Available at: https://www.bl.uk/romantics-and-victorians/ar ticles/perceptions-of-childhood#authorBlock1.

Ryan, R.M. and Deci, E.L. (2017). *Self-Determination Theory: Basic Psychological Needs in Motivation, Development, and Wellness.* New York: Guilford Press.

Sutton-Smith, B. (2001). *The Ambiguity of Play.* Cambridge, MA: Harvard University Press.

Warr, P.B. (2019). *The Psychology of Happiness.* Abingdon: Routledge.

White, J. (2007). *Playing and Learning Outdoors.* London: Routledge.

Green is good

DOI: 10.4324/9781003137023-1

Wellbeing themes in this chapter:

Belonging…Mindfulness…Physical movement…Resilience…
Connectedness…Senses…Restoration

"Inside is stuffy. Outside there are no limits. You can just run free."
Emily

Introduction

"What would our lives be like if our days and nights were as immersed in nature as they are in technology?" *(Richard Louv, 2012)*

We all need to feel connected to nature in order to feel good and function well (Richardson et al., 2019), and regular opportunities to play in nature improve children's emotional wellbeing, particularly if the environment includes 'wild' spaces rather than just adult-friendly manicured outdoor areas.

You're much more likely to see deeper engagement in natural spaces that are less 'managed' because nature provides complex exploration opportunities that are difficult to replicate. When we enable children to 'go wild,' they get sensory feedback from long grasses and feel joy at splashing in puddles. They improve their fine  motor skills from picking weeds and work on their proprioception skills by tackling different gradients. They experience increased freedom and independence in secret spaces and develop spatial awareness by swinging from branches. Even in settings where there is limited access to wild areas, we can still enable nature to nurture children, as you will see.

Healthy mind...

"Being outside lets you relax your brain." Emily

If you imagine a place that brings you peace, you're probably thinking of a natural space. When I feel overwhelmed, I pull on my walking boots and walk until I feel calm again. Even as little as five minutes of 'green exercise' can improve mood and self-esteem (National Trust, 2020), and 'nature connectedness' is linked to lower depression and  anxiety levels (National Trust, 2020). Biologist Edward O. Wilson proposed that we're drawn to nature because in the past it helped us survive (Wilson,

23

1984). Our wellbeing is intricately connected with nature – perhaps we can see children's need to play with water and soil, and their fascination with fire, as an instinctive urge to connect with what nourishes them.

I remember once feeling so overwhelmed that I had to stop my car on a bridge over a river. I was struggling with my mental health due to the stressful nature of my job at the time, and this was affecting my physical health too. As I looked out over the gently moving water, two swans emerged from under the bridge and drifted slowly down the river. Focusing on this scene gave me the sense of perspective I needed, and I felt the weight lifting from my shoulders. I resolved to find a different job and handed in my notice shortly afterwards.

Attention restoration theory

The impact of natural environments on mood, state of mind, and health has been studied by Professors Rachel and Stephen Kaplan for over 20 years. They've concluded that time in nature helps our brains recover from stress and also improves focus and concentration. Their attention restoration theory (ART) suggests that our attention is divided into two parts – directed and involuntary – and interactions with a natural environment allow our directed attention to rest. Studies have found that a 20-minute walk in a park restores attentional fatigue for many children with ADHD, producing effects similar to those of Ritalin (Faber Taylor and Kuo, 2009). According to attention restoration theory, there are four stages of attention along the way to recovery:

- Clearer head or concentration. At this stage, we let go of thoughts, worries, and concerns that are demanding our attention.
- Mental fatigue recovery. We can feel drained and mentally exhausted by activities that require focused and directed attention, and this stage allows directed attention to recover and to be restored to normal levels.
- Soft fascination or interest. A low-stimulation activity enables us to be gently distracted

and engaged, reducing the internal noise and providing a quiet internal space to relax.

- Reflection and restoration. We're able to relax, restore our attention, and focus on what really matters by spending a longer period of time in an appropriate natural environment (Kaplan and Kaplan, 1989).

Without this time in nature, our stress and fatigue levels are likely to increase. Children do need the opportunity to run, jump, climb, and ride bikes, but they also benefit from a mindful approach outdoors. Co-regulation is essential for very young children who are learning to regulate their emotions, or older children who struggle with this, and engaging in mentally restorative activities outside together is valuable.

TIME TO REFLECT:

Can you recall a time when you went through these stages? Can you picture yourself in that natural environment? Perhaps you have a place that you visit regularly to clear your mind and find peace?

Mindfulness outdoors

One wet and windy morning, I took a nursery class out to their Forest School area. As we tramped across the school field, located in the middle of a housing estate, a buzzard with a wingspan almost the size of a child's outstretched arms landed on the grass in front of us. We stood transfixed by the sight of the bird manoeuvring a bloodied rabbit more firmly into its talons. We were suddenly oblivious to the noise of traffic around us. A few moments later, the bird took off, eyeing us with cold disdain.

Mindfulness is about being fully present and engaged in the moment, and these activities can help:

- String walk: tie a length of string between two trees (or objects). If possible, the area below the string should include different gradients and terrain. Give each child a blindfold and ask them to follow a piece of string to its conclusion. The children get sensory feedback from the string, acoustic sounds, the tree bark, long grasses, and low dips in the ground.

- Cloud watching: this is a great way to distract the mind from stresses and worries. Once you draw children's attention to it, they will see that a cloudy sky often changes very rapidly. It's particularly satisfying to watch clouds on the horizon in autumn or winter – they can look like ever-changing cities. Gavin Pretor-Pinney, founder of the Cloud Appreciation Society, points out that we hardly even notice clouds unless they obstruct the sun.

> The bad press that clouds get is totally unfair. Clouds are in fact the most diverse, evocative, poetic aspect of nature. They remind us that we are creatures that inhabit this ocean of air. We don't live beneath the sky; we live within it. The digital world conspires to make us feel perpetually busy. Slowing down and being in the present, not thinking about what you've got to do, what you should have done, just being here, letting your imagination lift from the everyday concerns. It's good for you.
>
> (Pretor-Pinney, 2013)

- Sit spot: this was an activity that I was shown on my Forest School course. Children and adults find their own special spot and sit there quietly. Very young children may only be able to do this for a few seconds at first, but you can gradually build up the time. Encourage children to listen carefully and concentrate on what they can feel. It's good to go back to the same spot each time, building up that sense of belonging and noticing changes through the seasons.
- Leaf threading: find two twigs about the length of your index finger. Cut a piece of string or wool and tie each end to one of the twigs. Collect a few leaves and then use one twig as a 'needle,' pushing it through the centre of each leaf. (The second twig stops the leaves falling off the string or wool.)

- Stone stacking: balancing stones or pebbles on top of each other develops hand-eye co-ordination, as well as perseverance and resilience. It's an activity that can be both calming and frustrating at the same time! This is particularly engaging for children who are interested in the 'connecting' schema. *(Schemas are repeated patterns of behaviours that reflect a child's interests).*

- Gratitude prayer flags:

Tibetan prayer flags look beautiful blowing in the wind, and their vibrant colours – blue, white, red, green and yellow – represent the sky, air, fire, water and earth.

Tibetans believe that the wind carries the prayers printed on the flags, spreading goodwill and positive energy. An adaptation of this is to create gratitude flags. Expressing gratitude makes you happier and positively impacts on those around you. Ask the children to draw things they are grateful for on colourful squares of material, and then hang the flags in the outdoor space to enhance their sense of belonging.

- Fire: being in a fire circle helps build a sense of togetherness. I have a weekly fire in my setting. If you don't have much outdoor space, a temporary fire bowl need not take up much room.

TIME TO REFLECT:

Children are instinctively mindful, noticing what is around them. Do you allow yourself opportunities during the day to stop and notice?

...Healthy body

"It's more healthy outdoors." Emily

Children who move better, feel better, and evidence has shown that physical activity can alleviate the symptoms of depression (Craft and Perna, 2004). Green spaces can also be protective, preventing and reducing some chronic diseases. For example, asthma affects 1 in 11 children in the UK (Asthma UK, 2016), and increased tree cover is linked to a reduction in asthma rates in young children (Lovasi et al., 2008).

Children are generally more active outdoors, and they have increased freedom to move in different ways. This causes the brain to produce more serotonin, which regulates happiness levels: physical activity makes children happier!

A wild space provides a variety of natural obstacles, excellent for prompting different types of physical movement: jumping, clambering, crawling, sliding, rolling, climbing. Children tend to be more engaged by negotiating obstacles in a natural setting than indoor gym equipment. Obstacles, by their very nature, are a challenge, and, as Oprah's  famous saying goes: "challenges are gifts," helping children build up physical and emotional resilience.

To provide natural obstacles in a small space, consider:

- Long logs laid on the ground and short log sections standing up.
- Large sticks and branches.
- 'Jungle' type plants in pots.
- Different levels created by using small sections of railway sleepers.
- 'Gullies' with stones to define the edges. Fill with sand or woodchip.
- A straw bale (this can get messy!).

TIME TO REFLECT:

The full quote from Oprah Winfrey is: "challenges are gifts that force us to search for a new centre of gravity. Don't fight them. Just find a new way to stand." Can you think of times in your role when you have had to find a new way to stand? What was your motivation?

Sensory dysfunction

"What do you like about nature?" "What is nature? Oh, I like nature, climbing trees, getting dirty." Jack

A lack of outdoor play can lead to sensory dysfunction, where children fail to develop their full sensory abilities (Hanscom, 2016). There seems to have been a rise in the number of children who are presenting with sensory needs and, as time goes by, I teach increasing numbers of children who are clingy, nervous, or uncomfortable in natural spaces. One pupil was visibly distressed when walking on the varying surfaces in our outdoor area and it took a long time for her to feel comfortable walking on surfaces other than tarmac.

The antidote to sensory dysfunction is allowing children time and freedom to explore nature at their own pace. (It can be useful in the short term to allow an anxious child to bring something familiar from home or the classroom.) Children need time climbing trees, playing in muddy puddles, swinging, walking barefoot, and den building, to engage and improve all their senses (Hanscom, 2016). These senses include proprioception (the ability to sense what different parts of your body are doing without looking) and the vestibular sense (your body's GPS system which tells your body where you are and where you need to go).

Language development

If children's communication skills are significantly delayed, they can struggle to make friends and experience increased anger and frustration. They can feel isolated. Studies show that a child with poor vocabulary at the age of five is more likely to suffer mental health problems (Blanden, 2006) and, unfortunately, over 10% of UK children have long-term speech, language, and communication needs (NHS England, 2019). Natural outdoor environments have a more positive effect on the quality of children's speech and language than indoor spaces (Richardson and Murray, 2017), and they are an ideal springboard for vocabulary building because they evolve all the time. (If you have no wild space, you could consider local expeditions.)

Educational psychologist Dr Meredith Rowe has conducted a study of children's vocabulary, and she found that the quantity of words that adults use with children is not the whole story:

- At the age of 18 months, more input is better, and joint attention (where both the adult and the child are looking at the same thing) and gesture also help.
- At the age of 30 months though, children need more sophisticated and diverse vocabulary. Children have generally had more exposure  to commonly used words and have built up a vocabulary base. Using 'rare' words during interactions had a significant impact when children's vocabulary was measured one year later.
- At the age of 42 months, children benefit from narratives, where the past or the future are explored, and explanations, where 'why questions' are answered and explored (Rowe, 2012).

An important lesson from the study is that we need to expose children to words that are slightly beyond their level. It's clear that scaffolding the language during outdoor play needs to be different at different stages. We also need to remember that some of the older children in our care may have missed out on vital stages of vocabulary building.

Tips for language building outside:

- Model positional language: "Look, the squirrel is *on* the branch!"
- Use real binoculars or DIY ones made from toilet rolls to 'spot' things and describe them.
- Play nature scavenger hunt games.
- Sing and practise rhymes outside.
- Provide den building equipment and loose parts for construction to stimulate children to give instructions and follow them.
- Have an outdoor role play area: put out fabric, hats, scarves, shirts, dresses, bags (shopping bags, backpacks, handbags, suitcases), wallets, and purses. (Children absolutely love purses and wallets. They stimulate great discussion.)
- Go on a listening walk outdoors and talk about what you can hear.

- Include intriguing elements in the outdoor area. (For example, watching birds in a bird bath requires quiet and can help less confident children have a voice.)

Conversations during outdoor play can offer unique insights into children's thinking processes. For example, I was intrigued to see one of my pupils pushing wires from an old phone into the ground. "What are you doing?" I asked. "Oh," she replied, "I'm making sure the worms have electricity!"

Naming things is powerful and helps build a sense of belonging to the natural environment. Children love browsing through Collins Little Gems books, naming the birds and animals they know. To avoid confusion between different languages, scientific names are assigned to plants and animals, and children find some of these fascinating. For example, the scientific name for gorilla is 'gorilla gorilla gorilla,' a cat is 'felis catus,' and the black rat is known as 'rattus.' My favourite scientific name to share with young children is that of the bumblebee: 'bombus' (which means 'booming').

TIME TO REFLECT:

For a moment, put yourself in the place of a child who struggles day-to-day with communication. What emotions might that child be experiencing when playing with peers?

Ecological identity

Jan White, thinker and writer on outdoor play, believes that we have a reciprocal relationship with nature – if we look after nature, it looks after us. Nature, White believes, is a play partner for children, and children form an attachment to nature because it fulfils a psychological need (White, 2014).

Table 1.1 Jan White's play mapping

Appleton's survival needs	Examples of children's play behaviour
Refuge: having a safe secret place you can withdraw to and avoid danger.	Den making
Prospect: getting as high as possible in order to be able to see danger coming.	Tree climbing, balancing, play at different levels.
Trail: journeying, exploring, navigating, mapping out.	Making trails with natural resources and props such as rope or chalk.
Source: looking for things for survival such as water, food, den-making equipment.	Foraging or collecting, treasure hunts.

White was inspired by the work of Sobel (2008), Pelo (2013), and Appleton (1975). Appleton proposed that when we enter a new environment, we look to see if it meets our needs for survival. Appleton identified four needs that we have in a new natural environment and White has mapped these onto children's play and established strong links with schemas. For example, humans seek refuge in a new natural environment and we see this in children's den making. You can see Jan White's play mapping in Table 1.1.

TIME TO REFLECT:

When watching outdoor play, see if you can spot play behaviours that link with Jan White's play mapping. Are there aspects of the play mapping that are difficult for children in your setting?

Competence and confidence

"Do you learn new things outside?" "No, mammy, that's silly, I just roll down the hill and get muddy and have fun." Connie

As well as nurturing children, wild spaces act as one big provocation, inviting children to find out what they're capable of and test things out. (One of the

fascinating things about working with young children is that their capabilities change so rapidly.) Enabling children to access wild spaces helps them build physical and emotional competence (and this space doesn't need to be big for a very young child!).

It can be tempting to step in and solve problems for children who are struggling in the outdoor environment, especially when time is an issue, but we need to be careful that our impatience doesn't prevent children from learning to navigate difficulties. I have to confess that I find it frustrating helping all children get into wellies and salopettes on the first rainy day in September, but most children want to be out playing in the rain and are highly motivated to learn this important new skill. Ann Masten's concept of 'ordinary magic' leading to resilience was developed through a scheme called 'Project Competence' and I definitely see my outdoor space as a project competence training ground.

A study by the Wildlife Trust found that 84% of children who took part in regular outdoor activities felt capable of new things when they tried (Wildlife Trust, 2019). Highly resilient children are usually more competent and also positive about themselves and life in general (Souri and Hasanirad, 2011). Adults with low levels of resilience, on the other hand, are more likely to resort to unhealthy and destructive coping mechanisms. Having high expectations of children outdoors builds their coping strategies for now and for later life.

Children are not robots, and they all learn in different ways and at a different pace, so a challenge in a natural environment won't be the same for every child. It might be climbing a tree for one child, whereas for another child, it could be allowing a woodlouse to crawl on their hand. For another child it might simply be feeling the wind on their face.

The child in the images on the following page was initially fearful about coming down the slope and wanted an adult to help her down. This was a good opportunity for critical thinking – evaluating the situation and making sound judgements. We talked about how she was feeling, and I reassured her that I was right there and could hold her hand if necessary.

Supportive relationships are key to developing competence and resilience. Communication is crucial to critical thinking, and we talked about the problem together – she was 'stuck' and too scared to stand up. Modelling by peers can be valuable, and another child climbed up beside her and then he ran down. Although she didn't feel able to copy this, it gave her confidence, and she decided to adjust the challenge by sliding down on her bottom. She was exhilarated at having achieved this and climbed up again and again until she was able to come down on her feet. Being able to talk through the process and reflect on it helped her then coach other children. Children often need to repeat actions over and over again to gain mastery of them, and we don't always allow them enough time. (You can see in Chapter 4 how much more confident this child became over the following few months!)

TIME TO REFLECT:

What prevents children from developing resilience?

Barriers

"I wish they brought us outside because even if it was raining, it's not a big deal. It's only rain." Emily

Studies have found that many children spend less time outdoors than prison inmates (Persil, 2016), and author Richard Louv warns that children are experiencing 'nature deficit disorder' (Louv, 2005). This puts more pressure on us to give children as much access to outdoor play as possible, but it's not always straightforward. When I conducted an informal poll of early years settings, 20% of respondents said they could only allow access to the outdoors at certain times due to staffing issues. One teacher commented: "I work at a school that does forest school and we have a Montessori approach embedded in our provision, but we still struggle to open areas for outdoor learning due to staffing." I recently met a Reception teacher with no TA who has made a 'Play Pledge' in partnership with his pupils. They have agreed on a minimum time that the children can be outdoors each day (in addition to official break times). The Play Pledge ensures that he has made a commitment to outdoor play in difficult circumstances.

Testing and academic progress demands are also an issue. The Good Childhood Report 2020 found that UK children had the lowest levels of life satisfaction in Europe, partly caused by school-work pressures and "a particularly British fear of failure." Young people interviewed said they felt judged if they didn't succeed first time, and it feels as  though we're giving children the message that problem-solving and creative thinking are not valued: it's all about getting the answer on the test right first time.

Many practitioners told me that senior staff had insisted that access to outdoor play was sacrificed in favour of more adult-directed indoor learning. We need to consider what we're preparing children for and think beyond tests at age 5 or even at age 15. In partnership with parents and the wider society, we're teaching future community creators. What do we want these communities to look like? What will it feel like to be a citizen in these communities?

The biggest issue preventing outdoor play, according to my poll, is weather. We rarely suffer extreme weather in the UK, but some adults working with young children are wet weather averse, and children quickly pick up on negative body language. We need to convey to children that our changeable climate is a positive thing – so many sensory experiences available in a single day! Janine is a teacher at a nursery:

> Because it was so wet one year, everyone decided to get themselves a proper waterproof coat and a pair of waterproof trousers, and it was a huge mind shift. The staff were completely different. They felt more relaxed and got involved in a way that they would not have done before. It was such a small change but such a big impact.

Studies show that we can't support children's wellbeing effectively if our own emotional and social needs are not met (Weare and Gray, 2003) and investing in good-quality waterproofs will definitely help your wellbeing!

Dealing with complaints from parents and carers about children being outside in wet or cold weather can be stressful, and the best way to deal with this is to build strong relationships and be explicit about the benefits. Sharing children's enjoyment of playing in the sun, rain, snow, and wind is one of the most effective ways to get parents and carers on side.

Thirteen percent of the teachers who took part in my informal poll stated that a lack of adequate wet weather clothing for children was a real barrier. It's worth fundraising for a set of quality waterproofs – a good set won't need replacing for years.

The final barrier I want to explore is limited outdoor space, which is a real problem for many settings.

"We have no straightforward access to the outdoors, but we try to compensate with regular outdoor learning slots." Teacher

"Our playgrounds are both used continuously for playtime, PE and lunch breaks. Being inner city makes it hard as well. Curriculum demands also make it hard." Teacher

Bridgit Brown runs Pebbles Childcare in Worthing:

> We only have a small area of outdoor space available, so we do all we can to utilise our local environment and surrounding areas. We're lucky to be situated a stone's throw away from the beach as well as the South Downs, so the possibilities for outdoor exploration really are endless.

The journey to a different location can provide as much enjoyment as play at the destination, and when young children can move at their preferred pace, they can be playful with natural materials and enjoy different sensory experiences along the way.

Urban nature is still nature, and research has found that simply noticing the good things in urban nature each day is linked to sustained improvements in wellbeing (Richardson and Sheffield, 2017). It's also worth seeing the world from a young child's perspective: they can get green benefits from a tiny natural space.

Ben Tawil is co-director of a play consultancy called Ludicology:

> My second child was a keen explorer and one day she said "we've been playing in the woods! It's amazing in the woods!" I thought this was wonderful because I spent most of my childhood in the woods. As I talked to her about it, I realised she wasn't describing the woods; she was actually describing a rhododendron bush in the school yard. For a five-year-old, that's a forest. As adults, we can miss that: the 'woods' can literally be that carefully placed bush.

Six percent of respondents to my survey said they had no straightforward access to the outdoors. Sometimes it's necessary to be creative, as you will see in the following case study.

CASE STUDY: PART OF THE COMMUNITY

Bettina Sebak is the director of the German Kindergarten, a group of pre-schools in London whose ethos centres around learning through play close to nature. One of the nurseries, managed by Patricia Sokoll, is located within a typical inner-city housing estate and has virtually no outdoor space, just a small patio, a common issue for inner-city nurseries. The housing estate is a mixed-income community, with both social housing and expensive private apartments. In the centre is a communal garden which was seen as unsafe and rarely used by residents. However, Bettina and Patricia spotted potential in this green space sheltered by mature chestnut trees, and the team went round daily, picking up rubbish, removing cigarette butts and working with the community. Funds were raised for a playground and climbing frame. "We did a lot to fit in with our local neighbourhood, rather than impose ourselves," says Bettina, "it was important that we spoke to all the neighbours. That personal connection is much stronger than anything else. You need acceptance from the people around you."

Every day, Patricia and her team took a small group of children into this space to play. They put out a paddling pool, a trampoline, bikes and trikes and scooters. They created a mud kitchen and a sand-play area. They planted giant sunflowers and herbs. "We made ourselves heard and known," says Bettina. The nursery children became part of everyday life on the estate, and families began to see the community garden area as a play space, rather than a deserted, hostile space.

However, Bettina gradually became aware of another issue: drug dealing. The walkways through the estate were ideal delivery and escape routes, and nooks and crannies were used for hiding drugs. Bettina decided to take a "hands-on and direct German approach" to the problem and asked the drug dealers to leave, but this didn't work. The police had limited resources.

> What did work was putting play equipment out and hanging up the children's tiny wet swim suits. Suddenly the space was being used in a different way. Drug dealers don't want to conduct business in front of little children; they didn't feel comfortable with it. No-one does that, around children playing. So, the drug dealers left.

Bettina found that a simple action like children regularly playing outdoors changed the public perception of an urban outdoor space. Crime was reduced, and the community was strengthened. Bettina comments:

> The problem with some areas is that everyone lives in their own flat and no one knows each other. There is no cohesion or neighbourhood. We created a neighbourhood, a community. It is much better for children because they can play there, but it is also a communicative space for the estate. The more we're outside, the happier the children are, and it makes the work of the educators easier too because entertainment doesn't need to be provided, it's just there. Children are playing outdoors, and they have space and inspiration. They can be in a group, or they can be alone. It's their choice. Rather than sheltering the children from the local community, why not engage the residents and say: "these children are part of our community."

Making the connection

Belonging

An interesting exercise is to take the children outside and simply say these three words: "whose is this?" I have had very different answers from children in different settings. It can be enlightening to discover the level of ownership that children feel. Take a minute to think about the degree to which the children you work with understand that it is their space. (And do *you* feel it is their space?)

When children feel they 'belong' to an outdoor space, they feel included and see themselves as having a degree of power and control. Involving children in planning and planting helps them feel ownership.

Grow a sense of belonging:

- Remember that plants can grow in even the smallest outdoor area, enabling easy access to nature.
- Include a good diversity of plants to attract a wide range of minibeasts so that the play area is less sterile, more thera-peutic, and more eco-friendly.
- Support children to find and watch minibeasts so that they feel they 'fit in' and understand they are a powerful and influential part of this environment.
- Play games where children have to spot, identify, and match plants to increase a healthy nature connection.
- Provide different sized watering cans and gardening tools to get children hands on.
- Model traditional activities such as whittling to promote a sense of belonging. It's also an excellent opportunity to involve parents and grandparents who may know of local nature traditions that you haven't come across.

TIME TO REFLECT:

Do you remember any natural spaces you 'belonged' to as a child?

Sowing the seeds

Greening the play space helps children feel restored and stimulates their sensory system. Resilience is key – we need resilient plants as well as chil-dren! If you can let areas grow wild, simply throw down some wildflower seeds – these will thrive with minimum interference. A large patch of pop-pies is a real showstopper, and they are famously hardy. They attract bees and the dried seed heads make attractive play props. (The Food Standards Agency warns there's a slight risk of toxins from the sap and seeds, but a huge quantity would need to be consumed to cause illness.)

Drought-resistant plants such as succulents are ideal for a small space and survive well in containers. If you look at the planting around supermarkets or new housing developments, you'll often see shrubs, hostas, daylilies, sedum, astilbe, and achillea – all plants that do well with very little attention.

As well as surviving a lack of water, plants also need to survive children's play. Children instinctively have to touch everything, and this sensory feedback boosts their emotional wellbeing.

We're back to succulents again – they will withstand a great deal of rough treatment and will grow in any container. I even have them planted in old cake tins. Children interested in the transporting schema have dug up and moved whole sections and the succulents still thrive. A child from our nursery pulled out one succulent plant and put it in a closed wicker box. When it was discovered a few weeks later, it was still growing well!

"Mexican fleabane flowers for most of the year and will self-seed everywhere, filling cracks and looking resplendent between stepping stones. Children love picking the daisies and there are so many of them, they can pick, pick and pick away! It's very robust and you can literally tear bits off it." Teacher, Emma Wilkie

Herbs such as lavender, rosemary, and mint are equally robust and will withstand children snipping, tasting, and even rolling on them. When crushed, mint releases a mood-elevating scent – stimulating and relaxing at the same time. This can create a wonderfully mindful moment, distracting children from anxiety and stress. Another herb that is said to reduce stress is lavender, one of the most frequently used herbs in aromatherapy. To strengthen the nature connection, give children dried herbs and see if they can match them to the growing herbs. Herbs are wonderful for potion play – provide water, scissors, weighing scales, containers, stones for grinding, and different-sized spoons nearby. As long as you are allergy aware and have removed poisonous plants (or educated the children about them), the nature connection is boosted when children can tear and taste different plants.

Harvest while you play

Children love to 'forage,' and this connects them with the natural rhythms of nature. When schools first reopened more widely after the first COVID-19 lockdown, the children in my class were physically and mentally restored by spending time in the wilder area of the school site. They ate apples, raspberries, and blackberries as they played, being mindful not to strip the whole plant. It prompted meaningful discussions on healthy eating.

A few more edible plants to grow are:
- Beetroot. A beautifully coloured superfood. It's easy to grow and many children are unfamiliar with it, making it an attractive novelty. It also produces a wonderful natural dye that you can use for playdough.
- Rainbow chard. Another low-effort, high-reward plant. It's versatile and children enjoy the bright colours.
- Peas. Children enjoy watching them grow in pots and then snacking on the peas in the pod.
- Potatoes. Growing potatoes is like growing treasure! Children are so excited to harvest them. Make sure you plant earlies so they are ready before the summer holidays or a main crop that you can harvest when you return after the holidays.
- Cress. Easy to grow if you don't have access to outdoor space.

Help children to make plant labels to stick in the ground – ask them what they want to label (my pupils were keen to label the daisies!). Planning, planting, and growing are important life skills that help 'root' children in nature, and although gardening is not generally thought of as 'play,' it's often an activity that children choose to do outdoors. Studies show that gardening reduces anxiety and stress, as well as giving us a sense of purpose and worth (Mike Edmondstone, 2018).

Planting for physical wellbeing

Grass provides a softer landing than other artificial surfaces. You could also consider golden creeping Jenny, woolly thyme, and ajuga reptans. These are all suitable under a swing and offer some 'bounce' factor. Carpets of chamomile are another idea: soft, durable, scented, and no maintenance once established.

Grassed areas are great for running and barefoot walking. The vestibular system, which is fundamental to wellbeing, gets a good workout when children can roll and slide on grassed slopes. Logs, branches, and tree stumps are a great sensory provocation, improving fine and gross motor skills.

Besides short grass, long grasses offer hiding places, which can elicit feelings of both exhilaration and relaxation. When children are asked what they would change about their school, many mention spaces for escape or withdrawal (Korelek and Mitchell, 2005), and feeling they can elude adult surveillance is important to children. Children crave the 'hinterland,' those hidden areas lying beyond what is visible or known. Surely we all remember these adventures?

Ideas for growing hidden spaces:

- Bamboo is the fastest growing plant on earth and makes a good screen.
- Willow also grows quickly and can be manipulated to create structures.
- Plant a sunflower circle.
- Make a runner bean tipi. Arrange three canes in a tipi shape and secure them in the ground and at the top with twine. Plant a runner bean plant at the base of each cane. As they grow, secure the bean plants to the canes.
- Sticks and branches are great for den building, and trees such as alder, hazel, and birch grow quickly. Get the children to build a mini den first with twigs.

Water also features prominently when children are asked to design their own spaces, and pupils at one London school suggested that their school gardens should include ponds filled with frogs, and fountains for drinking and swimming (Korelek and Mitchell, 2005). At my setting, the children are intrigued by the frog life cycle evident in our pond. A bathyscope or aquascope enables children to get a really good view of the underwater world, and you can even make your own, using a plastic bottle.

Children are fascinated by water and studies show that 'blue space' can reduce stress and induce calm. If you don't have the room or inclination for a large-scale pond, you can create a mini pond within minutes by digging a shallow hole and placing a large tray or similar container at ground level. Birdbaths also create great fascination and are easy to make.

TIME TO REFLECT:

Can you think of ways to increase sensory engagement through outdoor play?

Conclusion

Being in nature is therapeutic and has been found to lower depression and anxiety. It engages children's senses and invites them to take appropriate risks and try things out.

During the COVID-19 pandemic, access to the outdoors was dramatically limited, and people suddenly showed an increased appreciation for nature. Public green spaces became essential, and nature reclaimed some urban areas. Welcoming wildlife into the outdoor space helps children remain connected to nature and builds healthy habits for life.

TIME TO REFLECT:

- Where do you go to feel restored and rejuvenated?
- Why would young children need a space to recover?
- How do you know that the children in your care feel a sense of belonging to the outdoor space?
- What type of sensory engagement opportunities are offered by your outdoor space?
- What responsibilities do the children have for planning, planting, and maintaining the space?
- How does the natural outdoor environment enable children to devise and 'solve' their own challenges?

References

 ## Reading for children

Booth, A. (2020). *Bloom*. London: Tiny Owl Publishing.
Cage, J., Cage, J. and Long, L. (2017). *Mud Book: How to Make Pies and Cakes*. New York: Princeton Architectural Press.

Covell, D. (2018). *Run Wild*. New York: Viking.

Ehlert, L. (2014). *Leaf Man*. New York: Houghton Mifflin Harcourt.

Jeffers, O. (2018). *This Moose Belongs to Me*. New York: Philomel Books, An Imprint of Penguin Book (USA) Inc.

Lindgren, A. (2014). *The Children of Noisy Village*. Oxford University Press.

Ray, M.L. and Stringer, L. (2009). *Mud*. Orlando: Voyager Books, Harcourt.

 Reading for adults

Asthma UK. (2016). *Asthma facts and statistics*. [online]. Asthma UK. Available at: https://www.asthma.org.uk/about/media/facts-and-statistics/.

Blanden, J. (2006). 'Bucking the trend': What enables those who are disadvantaged in childhood to succeed later in life? Available at: https://dera.ioe.ac.uk/7729/1/WP31.pdf.

Craft, L.L. and Perna, F.M. (2004). The benefits of exercise for the clinically depressed. *Primary Care Companion to the Journal of Clinical Psychiatry*, 06(03), 104–111. Available at: https://www.ncbi.nlm.nih.gov/pmc/articles/PMC474733/.

Edmondstone, M. (2018). Could gardening help the mental health of school children? [online]. *Learning Outside the Classroom*. Available at: https://learningoutsidetheclassroomblog.org/2018/12/10/could-gardening-help-the-mental-health-of-school-children/#:~:text=Gardening%20is%20one%20method%20that [Accessed 13 February 2021].

Faber Taylor, A. and Kuo, F. (2009). Children with attention deficits concentrate better after walk in the park. *Journal of Attention Disorders*, 12(5), 402–409. doi:10.1177/1087054708323000

Fairclough, M. (2020). *Wild Thing: Embracing Childhood Traits in Adulthood for a Happier, More Carefree Life*. London: Hay House UK Ltd.

Hanscom, A.J. (2016). *Balanced and Barefoot: How Unrestricted Outdoor Play Makes for Strong, Confident, and Capable Children.* Oakland: New Harbinger Publications, Inc.

Holland, C. (2012). *I Love My World: Mentoring Play in Nature, for Our Sustainable Future.* Otterton: Wholeland Press.

James, M. (2018). *Forest School and Autism A Practical Guide.* London: Jessica Kingsley Publishers.

Jarvis, P., Newman, S. and Swiniarski, L. (2014). On 'becoming social': The importance of collaborative free play in childhood. *International Journal of Play*, 3(1), 53–68. doi:10.1080/21594937.2013.863440

Kaplan, R. and Kaplan, S. (1989). *The Experience of Nature: A Psychological Perspective.* Cambridge University Press.

Knight, S. (2013). *Forest School and Outdoor Learning in the Early Years.* London: Sage.

Koralek, B. and Mitchell, M. (2005). The schools we'd like: Young people's participation in pre-school. In: Dudek, M. (Ed.), *Children's Spaces* (pp. 114–153). Oxford, UK: Architectural Press.

Kuo, F.E. and Faber Taylor, A. (2004). A potential natural treatment for attention-deficit/hyperactivity disorder. *Evidence from a National Study. American Journal of Public Health*, 94(9), 1580–1586.

Louv, R. (2005). *Last Child in the Woods: Saving Our Children from Nature-Deficit Disorder.* Chapel Hill: Algonquin Books.

Louv, R. (2012). *The Nature Principle: Reconnecting with Life in a Virtual Age.* Chapel Hill: Algonquin Books of Chapel Hill.

Lovasi, G., Quinn, J.W., Neckerman, K.M., Perzanowski, M., and Rundle, A. (2008). Children living in areas with more trees have lower prevalence of asthma. *Journal of Epidemiology and Community Health*, 62(7), 647–649. doi:10.1136/jech.2007.071894

National Trust. (2020). *Noticing Nature: First Report of the Noticing Nature Series.* [online] https://nt.global.ssl.fastly.net/documents/noticing-nature-report-feb-2020.pdf.

NHS England. (2019). *NHS England Speech, Language and Communication Services.* [online] www.england.nhs.uk. Available at: https://www.england.nhs.uk/ltphimenu/children-and-young-people/

speech-language-and-communication-services/#:~:text=More%20than%2010%25%20of%20all.

Persil. (2016). *Free the Kids.* [online] Available at: https://www.persil.com/uk/free-the-kids.html [Accessed 10 February 2021].

Pretor-Pinney, G. (2013). Gavin Pretor-Pinney: Cloudy with a chance of joy. *TED Conferences.* Available at: https://www.youtube.com/watch?v=lhP52caGW6s&ab_channel=TED [Accessed 3 March 2021].

Richardson, M., Hunt, A., Hinds, J., Bragg, R., Fido, D., Petronzi, D., Barbett, L., Clitherow, T. and White, M. (2019). A measure of nature connectedness for children and adults: Validation, performance, and insights. *Sustainability,* 11(12), 3250.

Richardson, M. and Sheffield, D. (2017). Three good things in nature: Noticing nearby nature brings sustained increases in connection with nature. *Psyecology,* 8(1), 1–32. doi:10.1080/21711976.2016.1267136

Richardson, T. and Murray, J. (2017). Are young children's utterances affected by characteristics of their learning environments? A multiple case study. *Early Child Development and Care,* 187, 3–4, 457–468. doi:10.1080/03004430.2016.1211116

Rowe, M. (2012). A longitudinal investigation of the role of quantity and quality of child-directed speech in vocabulary development. *Child Development,* 83(5), 1762–1774.

Souri, H. and Hasanirad, T. (2011). Relationship between resilience, optimism and psychological wellbeing in students of medicine. *Procedia: Social and Behavioral Sciences,* 30, 1541–1544.

The Wildlife Trust. (2019). Institute of Education [online]. Available at: https://www.wildlifetrusts.org/sites/default/files/2019-11/Nature%20nurtures%20children%20Summary%20Report%20FINAL.pdf [Accessed 13 February 2021].

Weare, K. and Gray, G. (2003). *What Works in Developing Children's Emotional and Social Competence and Wellbeing?* London: Department for Education and Skills.

White, J. (2014). *Being, Playing and Learning Outdoors: Making Provision for High Quality Experiences in the Outdoor Environment with Children 3–7*. New York: Routledge.

Wilson, E.O. (1984). *Biophilia*. Cambridge, MA: Harvard University Press.

Beneficial spaces

2

Introduction

"We play here, and we jump on trees and climb trees!" Cerys

The word 'beneficial' comes from the Latin word for kindness or service. How do we enable the outdoor space to be kind to children? It's tempting to spend lots of time looking at pictures of other people's outdoor spaces for inspiration, but for children's wellbeing, the

space needs to be made for them and with them.

There's a tendency to overthink it and focus too much on what looks good to other adults. Observe play at different times of the day, audit the space with the children, and see what is needed. (Bear in mind

DOI: 10.4324/9781003137023-2

Bob Hughes' types of play.) Get the local community involved to ensure it's a collaborative effort and that the space is part of its community. But most importantly, don't forget that the most important part of the outdoor space is you.

Who's it all for?

"How many schools have there been with a chain-link and black-top playground where there has been a spontaneous revolution by students to dig it up and produce a human environment instead of a prison?" (Simon Nicholson, 1971)

I was once employed on a play consultation scheme to give feedback to the council on why young people were repeatedly burning down the new playgrounds being installed. On our first evening there, my colleague and I met the local youth workers in the youth centre, a flat-roofed building in the centre of a run-down housing estate. Suddenly there was a loud banging and scrabbling in the darkness. A few minutes later, we heard a steady drumming above our heads that became almost deafening. The hairs on the back of my neck stood up. Then, after about ten minutes, the noise abruptly stopped. One of the youth workers turned to us and said: "they do that sometimes." The young people drumming their feet on the roof felt ignored and frustrated, and they'd felt like that for years.

Do we really listen to children's views? Teacher Ashleigh Robertson talks frankly about her own play journey, a journey that many of us can relate to:

"At the start of my teaching career I did do play, but I didn't do proper play – it was very structured. I'd have different zones, and those zones would look pristine and lovely. I'd have what I called 'play groups' and the children would go round in a rotation, spending maybe ten minutes at each station, not nearly enough time for them to get involved in play. Then I'd ring a bell, and they'd move onto the next play zone. I thought I was doing a really good job. But then I did reading and research and I realised this is not real play – the fact that we were telling them what to do at these zones. I'm not ashamed to admit that is the person I was.

I'm now in a position where I fully understand play, and my children have benefitted so much from me educating myself about it. I'm happy for them to lead it. They set up the play areas, they choose what we have. There are no time limits and children get to choose how long they play at a space because I know that play can't possibly happen in ten minutes – not deeply. There are no play groups, there's no bell ringing, it's all child led and fits in with their interests."

Ashleigh is one of the most skilled early years practitioners I know, and you can read more about her setting in Chapter 6.

Children are often given the message that the outdoor environment has been organised for their benefit and that they need to play in it in a certain way. An outdoor environment themed to a topic such as transport doesn't allow children much freedom or room for creativity because it's clear how children are 'supposed' to play. Open-ended provocations, on the other hand, can be interpreted in unanticipated ways by children (resulting in those wonderful moments we discuss enthusiastically when the children have gone home).

Children want responsibility, and they want to solve problems and tackle challenges. They want to be seen, and they want to believe that their ideas matter. By supporting them to develop decision-making skills, we help them navigate life's complexities.

Children's ideas were listened to and valued throughout 'Children Transforming Spatial Design,' a three-year research project led by Rosie Parnell. Children worked together with architects to tackle different design briefs, ranging from a playground installation to a school science pavilion (Birch, 2016a, 20016b). Although the process was not always straightforward, the children found it incredibly rewarding, and one landscape architect concluded that "children can handle virtually everything in a design process" (Birch et al., 2017).

TIME TO REFLECT:

Who is your outside space designed for and with?

Auditing the outdoor space for emotional wellbeing:
(As previously mentioned, the Leuven Scales work well for this.)

- Watch how children play – are there any obvious issues or regular sources of conflict? Are all children included in the way that they want to be? Are there permanent or temporary changes that need to be made to extend the play you see?

- Take time to be in the space with the team and without the children and talk about what it feels like to be in each area. What opportunities are there?
- Are there enough quiet, withdrawal spaces? Are they working effectively?
- Are there opportunities for children to collaborate and build social skills? For example, sand, loose parts, den building, role play, small world.
- Are children able to interact with natural elements?
- Are there opportunities for children to move in different ways on different surfaces?
- Are there meaningful opportunities for children to build competence and confidence? For example, a gardening area with real, child-sized tools or a woodwork bench.

Now ask the children to give you a tour…

Through the child's eyes

Conducting an audit with the children is the best way to find out how they see the space, and it doesn't need to be a complicated process. When children feel listened to, this develops their sense of belonging, which can act as a buffer against the effects of disadvantage (Anna Freud Centre, 2020). A child-led audit can also stimulate great discussion amongst staff.

Because children know every stone and bush, they have a unique perspective. When they give a tour of the space, how do they refer to each area? Which areas are they enthused by? Are there areas they are wary of?

My class were thrilled to hear that we were filming a tour of our outdoor space for a Reception class based in France. The places chosen by the children and their explanations were interesting:

"It's a hill and sometimes we roll down it and sometimes we hide behind it."

"There's a dragon. It flies."

"This is our big sandpit, and I like running across the top of it."

"We've got the big cable reels and I hide them. I roll them and hide them."

"I like playing in this bit. You can run and … you can jump!"

"We put our hands on it (string) and, you can walk along."

"This is the log cabin. We put our salopettes on here and after we put our boots on."

"A fire goes out with water here!"

"I like hiding here sometimes and sometimes people are chasing me."

"I like eating under the hill and having cake. I like hiding there and making stuff really nice. I like having tea parties there with cake and real tea and cake. Just here, in this bit."

"I play hide and seek here!" (Climbing frame.)

"I like to jump in the air." (Lays a piece of wood across a muddy puddle and jumps on the wood.)

"We put the wood over here (gap in the bench within a wooden structure) and then walk over the bridge."

"I put them (cable reels) here and climb up them then I climb inside (wooden structure) and go round and do it again! It's good and it's scary!"

"My best bit is here. There's a puddle, and there's a fish in there." "Where?" "I saw it, look, there…"

The puddle had formed over the previous two days and was around 3 ft wide and 3 inches deep. The children gazed into the dirty water, caught up in the magic. The first child to have 'spotted' the fish caught my eye to see if I might challenge him. I smiled and asked what the fish looked like. "I saw its tail!" interrupted another child, "Look! There!" Deciding that a newly formed puddle should be part of the tour demonstrates that my class don't view their play environment in terms of the fixed equipment and different zones but rather in terms of the opportunities it affords them at that very moment in time.

Back in 1988, Professor Harry Heft wrote that children view a space in terms of what they can do there rather than how it looks (Heft, 1988). Heft highlights that children may view a flat, smooth surface in terms of its possibilities for walking, running, cycling, and skateboarding. Where we see a fence

as a boundary, children see this as a climbing opportunity. Heft cites research by Robin Moore who asked children to draw maps of local areas. The children showed him places to climb, hide, slide, jump, and swing, and they referred to places as "the sliding hill" or "the house with the dog that bites" (Moore in Heft, 1988).

So children are less worried about what a space looks like and more concerned with the possibilities it offers. This means that the outdoor play space that best fulfils their needs might not look very photogenic. Sometimes we have to ignore our anxiety about how other adults might judge the outdoor space and simply tune into what our children need.

TIME TO REFLECT:

When arranging for children to give a tour of the area, how might you ensure that the 'quietest' voices are heard?

'Placeness: the quality of having or occupying a place'

The use of the word 'placeness,' meaning having or occupying a place, is now rare, but I've decided to reclaim it. How thoroughly do children occupy their outdoor space?

Children are driven to put their mark on their environment, and they enjoy having responsibility for it. Make them custodians – young children love to be included and relish the opportunity to get materials out and put them away; check loose parts for signs of damage; compost, dig, plant, and water.

At my setting, we have a discussion on a Friday about what should be outside during the following week, and the children have become sophisticated at mentally planning out the space and justifying and defending their decisions.

To ensure everyone feels a sense of placeness, it's a good idea to divide up the outdoor area so that ball play and bikes can carry on alongside outdoor small world play and drawing with chalk. Try giving children equipment to make temporary barriers. It's fascinating to see which zones they want, and children start to see that sometimes there has to be a negotiation process to make sure that everyone is included.

To ensure that barriers such as disability, gender, or race don't prevent 'placeness,' we should assess the space in terms of Universal Design, which aims to make things accessible to everyone without the need for adaptations or specialised designs (National Disability Authority, 2018). There are seven principles, which you can see in Table 2.1.

Table 2.1 The principles of universal design

Principle 1	Equitable use	The play space is accessible and appealing to all, and no children are stigmatised or segregated.
Principle 2	Flexibility in use	Children with a wide range of individual preferences and abilities can participate.
Principle 3	Simple and intuitive use	Regardless of experience, knowledge, language skills, or education level, the play space makes sense.
Principle 4	Perceptible information	The children using the play space understand everything they need to.
Principle 5	Tolerance for error	Hazards are minimised.
Principle 6	Low physical effort	The play space can be used effectively and comfortably with a minimum of fatigue.
Principle 7	Size and space for approach and use	Appropriate size and space is provided for approach, reach, manipulation, and use regardless of user's body size, posture, or mobility.

Play spaces that adhere to these principles are more likely to be inclusive. Most of all though, *we* make the biggest difference to enabling all children to participate.

Place attachment

Studies show that place, identity, and wellbeing are closely connected (Jack, 2015), and I still feel a strong sense of belonging to the school playground at my first school: the places where we play as children help shape us and make us who we are. If you think back to your childhood, the memories of outdoor play are probably most vivid because play engages so many different senses (Morgan, 2009). During times of stress, we sometimes mentally return to these childhood play places, pulling on a virtual comfort blanket. I took on the role of Head of School at the school I attended as a child so I knew every inch of the outdoor area. Sometimes, when I felt overwhelmed by the job, I would have dreams of being a child back in that playground which was odd but also comforting!

On the day I started that job, a four-year-old pupil asked me shyly "do you know where the secret hiding place is outside?" "Yes," I replied, "because I went to this school!" We then went straight out to find it together. I was first shown this area by older children, who probably learned about it from their older peers.

Why not find out where children's special outdoor places are? What do they call these places? If possible, ask parents and grandparents who attended the setting the same thing. Why not show children that we care about what they care about?

The following case study focuses on Chelsea Open Air Nursery, a place that has always been very firmly occupied by the children.

CASE STUDY: A TAPESTRY THAT GOES ON

Kathryn Solly was Headteacher of the renowned Chelsea Open Air Nursery School for nearly 17 years. The building dates back to 1587, and in 1928, early years pioneer Dr Susan Isaacs was involved in establishing an open-air nursery on the site. Today the pupils still play outdoors within the same walled garden.

When Kathryn took over, there was a great deal of work to be done because the school had been severely neglected. "I was insistent that we had to get things right for the children," says Kathryn, "they had to be safe and happy, and they had to have the right provision for their own levels of development."

The first priority was health and safety. A poisonous laburnum tree was removed from the school garden, and a deep uncovered well was made safe. Another safety issue was that old playground equipment had been removed, but the metal bases had been left. The team also had to deal with a dangerous bridge made of scaffolding poles.

Once the safety issues were resolved, an action plan was devised for the garden. Kathryn comments:

> I didn't want to destroy the good qualities that were there. Although it was a small space, it was enclosed, so it had that natural security, and it also had several trees that were protected and needed to be treated with respect. When you have a building of that age, changes have to be made sympathetically.

Landscape architect Helle Nebelong talks of the 'genius loci,' the spirit of a place, the qualities and atmosphere already present. This could be part of a building, a tree with character, or even something that happened there, and Nebelong states that this is an important starting point when designing a space (Nebelong, 2002).

During the planning stage, Kathryn drew on some of the fundamental beliefs of Susan Isaacs, including the importance of curiosity, imagination, symbolism, and also the idea of children as deeply social creatures. Kathryn wanted it to be a space that stimulated the imagination of children and so included as many natural materials as possible. Outside cover was seen as essential, particularly for babies.

Kathryn was adamant that the process was not about making decisions *for* the children: consultation was essential. Kathryn says:

> We needed to start at the beginning, and the beginning was the children. Their ideas were the embroidery on a tapestry. Every garden for children that I've been involved with has been a tapestry

that goes on: a garden never stays the same. The children change, the circumstances change, and so does a garden.

The adults talked with the children and showed them pictures from catalogues so that they could discuss the things they liked and consider how these things might be made to work in a relatively small space. Kathryn believes strongly that we must see the indoor and outdoor environment from a child's perspective. Architects working on the interior were asked to sit down on the floor with the children. "They became children," says Kathryn, "it's important to be at their level. If you're not careful, all children see is legs: table legs and human legs. And there is so much clutter inside and out." This technique was applied to the design of the outside space too, with the garden development team sitting on the ground and in a range of different places to get the child's perspective.

Kathryn and her team carried out an audit, mapping out the 'honey-pot areas' frequently used by the children:

> You audit for what you want to look at in terms of areas, and the usage of those areas. You can look at that usage in terms of gender, age profile, resources, as well as different times of the day, different times of the year, different weather.

What was eventually created by Kathryn and her team is what she calls "a garden for the imagination," filled with engaging elements such as a large sandpit, a vegetable patch, a firepit and mud kitchen, a pond, slides and seesaws, and climbing equipment. A calming oasis in a busy area of London.

When Kathryn showed parents round, she was able to tell in the first five minutes whether or not they would sign their children up.

> It was better to show parents round in winter because then they could see it warts and all. I would promise them several things: rain and all sorts of weather are conditions for being outside; getting dirty is part of childhood; grazing your knees is part of childhood. If you sign up for that, your child will have a real childhood here; they will flourish, grow and prosper. You could see some parents falling in love with it.

An environment that invites, fascinates, and engages

"Do not go where the path may lead, go instead where there is no path and leave a trail." Ralph Waldo Emerson

What invites children into an outdoor space? It could be fresh snowfall, rendering the space new and unrecognisable, or it could be the intimacy of a well-known space, drawing children in and enveloping them. When children are interested and absorbed by an environment, they experience the same happiness we do as adults when a physical space engages us. Once, while breathlessly hiking up a mountain in Colorado (being overtaken by tiny children who were used to the high altitude), I came across a beautiful lake surrounded by trees. The view mesmerised me but also evoked feelings of familiarity. Here I was, back in the thicket of trees around a pond I played in as a child, just on a much larger scale. Everything about the scene made me want to explore further – the dense woodland, clear water dotted with stepping stones, the cave-like structures created by huge boulders. Basically, I wanted to play!

Children are drawn to spaces with multiple play possibilities rather than beautifully manicured areas, and there needs to be a balance between spaces that are cluttered and confusing and adult-friendly spaces that offer no challenge at all. The Kaplans propose that mystery in a landscape invites people in, so, if there is room, why not create different zones to encourage healthy restorative interest and incorporate hidden surprises to invite fascination?

In a previous career, I designed and ran a project in the village of Mordiford focusing on the local legend of a child rescuing a baby dragon that grows into a bloodthirsty creature. One of the physical outcomes of the project was a set of bird boxes depicting parts of the legend, decorated by children and 'hidden' at different levels in the nearby woods. Every child visiting the woods noticed something different about the boxes, and the story of the dragon was a great play provocation.

It can be effective to borrow ideas from garden designers to help create 'mystery.' (Even better if the ideas are stimulated by the interests of the children.)

- Create intriguing pathways.
- Make child-sized tunnels by training beans or peas over hoops.
- Install a secret cave.
- Have a gate that appears to go nowhere.
- Put in a low wooden bridge over grass.
- Partly conceal a mannequin – or just the legs!
- Create a rockery, complete with tiny houses.
- Incorporate a disused boat into the play space.
- Install a water wall or bubble fountain.
- Plant up an old bike.
- Create large silhouettes of the children jumping and running and paint these onto walls or fences.

There's a 'dragon' in my current setting – a long, raised slope. Every child is fascinated by it, and they engage with it in multiple ways. Children will clamber up the slope, hauling on the grass to pull themselves up, slide down the muddy gullies, and run along the dragon's 'spine.' As each child enters the area, they shout hello to the dragon, and this feature helps them feel they belong. (After returning to school after lockdown in 2019, one child joyfully shouted "Oh! You're still here, dragon!")

TIME TO REFLECT:

Can you think of ways to incorporate intriguing or surprising elements in the outdoor space that build on children's interests?

An environment that invigorates

"He pushed me in the wheelbarrow, all on the bumpy bits! Then I pushed him. He pushed me and I pushed him!" Jamal

I once visited a setting where the outdoor landscape was completely flat with just a wooden castle that the children were rarely allowed to play on. Staff complained bitterly that the children were frequently fighting and often tried to hide "where they aren't allowed." The practitioners hated being outside because the children were continually "fussing and falling out with each other." It was obvious that the children were bored and frustrated – there was no potential for them to be deeply involved, wallowing in ideas, feelings, and relationships (Bruce, 2004).

In contrast, an outdoor area that galvanises children and provides mental and physical challenge is much more likely to ensure absorption in play.

Loose parts in the outdoor space work perfectly in this sense, and this is covered in depth in the next chapter.

Children are instinctive explorers, engaged by wild spaces, natural obstacles, and sensory-rich provision. In terms of healthy minds and bodies, it's hard to beat the wilderness, and a sterile playground can be completely transformed by re-wilding, and by adding slopes and dips, secret places and dens.

I once overheard my husband, a financial advisor, discussing 'productive uncertainty.' Later that day, watching children scrambling over a pile of logs, exploring a freshly iced pool of water, and digging in a pile of fallen leaves, this phrase came back to mind. Children need an element of productive uncertainty outdoors for wellbeing.

There are now well-thought out fixed play structures available, but off-the-shelf equipment can prevent children from developing physical skills and an appropriate recognition of risk. Danish landscape architect, Helle Nebelong, states that standardised playgrounds where there is an equidistant distance between the rungs in a climbing net or on a ladder can actually cause harm: "the child has no need to concentrate on where he puts his feet. Standardisation is dangerous because play becomes simplified, and the child doesn't have to worry about his movements" (Nebelong, 2002). A simple wooden platform offers more possibilities than a generic pirate ship or castle and promotes better language development. (This option is often cheaper too!)

A play space with flexibility is the best way to meet the physical and emotional development needs of children, and observations of play show us what is needed. This week, I saw that a child wanted to join others jumping off a wooden platform but was anxious, backing away again when he reached the edge. I brought out an agility table and mats, and we talked about techniques. Initially, he lost his nerve at the last minute and fell onto the mat, but he gradually gained the confidence to jump away from the equipment. He felt such a huge sense of pride in his new skills.

If space allows, children need different surfaces and gradients to practise jumping, running, rolling, and balancing. Grassy slopes encourage children to put their whole bodies into tackling the ascent and descent.

Tips for providing 'productive uncertainty':

- If there is grass, allow some wilderness! Have no-mow areas.
- Movable metal A-frames are fantastic for combining with loose parts such as planks. Ladders and balance beams help children build physical skills as well as focus, concentration, and determination.

- Create a 'stream,' using stones to make a gully for water, or simply enable giant rain puddles to form by digging shallow holes. It depresses me when children are banned from playing in puddles.
- Incorporate different textures such as woodchip, grass, sand, dirt.
- Fix upturned logs in the ground for stepping. A felled tree trunk is ideal for clambering and balancing.
- Have an area of boulders for climbing.
- Create banks and slopes (use hardcore, then cover this with topsoil and grass seed).
- Consider creating different 'islands' – sloped grassed areas.

TIME TO REFLECT:

Does your outdoor space include areas of 'productive uncertainty'?

An environment that challenges the senses

A mentally healthy outdoor space should offer plenty to engage children's senses because children need a well-functioning sensory system for good emotional wellbeing. Sensory play simulates new neurological connections as well as helping children make sense of the world around them.

For this reason, sand and dirt digging areas are essential. Children can easily transform sand, giving them a sense of control and experience of cause and effect. If possible, a sand pit should be big enough for children to get into, and you can create this fairly easily with wooden sleepers or even

just a tarpaulin with temporary barriers around the edge. Our sand pit is one of the most popular areas of the playground, and it is where friendships are formed, negotiations are made, and conversation is developed. Add 'bones' and 'fossils' to discover plus shells, pebbles, and tools.

Mud truly is glorious – such a fantastic open-ended, sensory resource. Having a dirt box promotes great social skills (there's plenty of teamwork while children dig to Australia!). Digging in the dirt can actually boost the immune system, and research shows that mud contains microscopic bacteria called *mycobacterium vaccae*, increasing levels of serotonin, which calms and relaxes (Lowry et al., 2007). Getting down and dirty in the mud makes children happier. Researcher Dr Chris Lowry comments:

> These studies help us understand how the body communicates with the brain and why a healthy immune system is important for maintaining mental health. They also leave us wondering if we shouldn't all spend more time playing in the dirt.
>
> (BBC News, 2007)

We need to get away from the idea that dirt is unhealthy, and allow children to get feet, hands, and even faces in the mud!

Mud kitchens stimulate great communication and, because they are such a crowd pleaser, children develop social skills such as sharing, listening, and co-operating. The 'cooking' in a mud kitchen – chopping grass, stirring water, kneading mud, adding herbs – can be a wonderfully mindful process. When children proudly present you with a delicious 'mud-n-worm' burger, just remember that they get a positive mental boost from preparing the 'food' and another from seeing their finished creation. Studies show that those who frequently complete small, creative projects report feeling more relaxed and happier in their everyday lives (Connor et al., 2018), and we can easily facilitate this in outdoor play. A brilliant way to increase belonging is to create mud faces together and stick them to tree trunks or fences. Sculpting mud is deeply satisfying, and my pupils love to make mud bricks, mud castles, and mud figures. Digging in the mud or sand and transferring it to a bucket or other container also helps children practise crossing the midline, an important developmental skill that helps with emotional regulation.

If you don't already own it, do buy *Mud Pies and Other Recipes*, by Marjorie Winslow. It's over 50 years old but remains a wonderful, funny, and charming book. Children are completely unfazed when they hear it is a cookbook for dolls, and they love following her (inedible) recipes and then inventing their own.

Seeing the wide range of play behaviours in our mud kitchen fills my heart with joy. You can see here the delight of a child who has discovered for the first time that this sink is different to the one at home – the water runs straight through the plug hole onto the ground!

Guttering is a great addition to a mud kitchen...

A sensory path for barefoot walking helps children develop balance, proprioception, and body awareness, and also works the fine motor muscles in the feet. It has been proved that children who spend more time barefoot have better control when they are running, climbing, and playing, and they are also more vigilant for hazards. Trentham Gardens is said to have the first barefoot path in the UK designed for families, and the 1 km length goes across straw, through mud, over cobble stones and log slices, through shallow streams, and over gravel and wooden sleepers. You can make a simple barefoot path using wood or bricks as dividers, and incorporating textures such as sand, chamomile, log slices, and pebbles. If space is an issue, a temporary barefoot path can be made using trays of sensory materials. From my experience, the children need absolutely no encouragement to try it out!

To engage children's sense of smell, you could consider complementing growing herbs with big water trays containing chopped up scented fruit such as oranges and lemons. The outdoor space lends itself to sensory, messy play such as painting with feet, water play, or cornflour play.

Water is both calming and stimulating. Children must be able to manipulate water in different ways: using tiny droppers, funnels, or water wheels in water trays; transporting water to different areas in buckets or other containers; washing with sponges and brooms; and getting soaked in the paddling pool or from hoses! One of our most popular donated loose parts is a large, unused home brewing container with a screw lid at the top and a tap at the bottom, and this has provoked lots of interesting play. Water is a true wellbeing booster.

TIME TO REFLECT:

How could sensory elements in play support inclusion?

A space to be calm

Some years ago, a child arrived from Syria to join my class. She did not speak and rarely interacted with others. Two weeks later, I heard her voice for the first time. She was with another child in a secret outdoor space well known to the children. As I peeked in, I could see that the two were lying in the little hollow of earth behind a bush. One was combing the other's hair. The new child asked, "are you my friend?" and the other replied "yes." There was silence for a few minutes then they began speaking about 'the ghost.' (There were white sheets in the outdoor dressing up box, and one child had decided he was a ghost, which had excited all the other children!) It took a few more days for the newly arrived child to speak in class, but she became close friends with the girl she spoke to in their secret place. An outdoor play area needs at least one quiet area, and these could be a combination of fixed structures and den-making equipment.

Do you recall the secret places you would hide in as a child, and that comforting feeling of being cocooned? The world can be a confusing place for young children, with many things to process, and secret hiding places offer comfort as well as a break from adult surveillance. When children who have emotional regulation difficulties feel calm and relaxed, this is the best time to discuss different emotions and how it feels to experience them. Quiet spaces such as dens can be particularly helpful for children in a high state of arousal.

The process of building a den is just as important for wellbeing as playing inside it, and there is often good conflict resolution and problem solving

involved. With frequent practise, I've found that even very young children can build effective dens, and a good starting point is to support children to lean branches or boards against a fence. Tarpaulins, shower curtains, and camouflage netting are all good for den building. You can make large dens by tying cord between trees, but children can independently make fantastic dens with crates or branches. If you can get hold of a few extra-large cardboard boxes, these work well but are less durable of course! Don't forget flooring – my pupils like to make dens on the tarmac as well as on the grass, and they use blankets and cushions inside. Hammocks are wonderful for mindful contemplation and can be especially calming for a child in a high state of arousal.

TIME TO REFLECT:

When you observe the children at play, are the quiet spaces working?

A space to be creative

"Making art allows children to glimpse their creative powers and reflect on the chaos of their lives." Grayson Perry

"Outdoor play is good for children because you can find cool things for art." Emily

Being able to express themselves creatively positively impacts on children's emotional wellbeing, and the outdoor space provides a much bigger platform and canvas. Loose parts play is one of the best ways to enable creativity, and the next chapter is dedicated to this subject. My outdoor role play space is a popular area, sheltered from the weather, and it generates some wonderful imaginative play. Listening to the conversations, I hear children trying out roles and exploring issues in their lives. They practise being someone different and test out new ideas and responses. Sometimes I'm invited into the scenario, which gives me useful insights into their thought processes. The children often bring their own props, such as pines cones, to this area.

Do you provide music outdoors? My class love to dance, and dancing boosts your mood and lowers stress, as well as building connections between people and strengthening muscles. Music itself can relax the mind and boost psychological wellbeing. Make sure children can make their own music outside too, with instruments or loose parts. If you grow your own bamboo, this provides multiple musical possibilities, from wind chimes to drumsticks.

In terms of art, children are usually clear on what they want to create and just need the choice of materials to achieve it. These could include:

- Large paper rolls.
- Fabric, string, and lengths of ribbon.
- Clipboards.
- Pencils and pens, chalk and charcoal.
- Large cardboard boxes to paint.
- Eco-friendly powder paint (or homemade powder paint).
- Big paintbrushes, rollers and sponges.
- Clay and tools.

Outdoor art provides the opportunity for children to work together with their peers in a way they can't inside and mess is much less of an issue. I love to see children lying on the ground outside, mark making. A playground covered in intricate chalk markings says: "we belong here."

The outdoor environment lends itself well to land art: art that is made directly in the landscape by sculpting the land itself or by making structures in the landscape with natural materials. You can show the children artwork by Andy Goldsworthy and Ugo Rondinone to inspire them. Land art makes connections between nature and art and could include mandalas, ice or snow art, wrapping trees with fabric, or using stones and leaves. Make sure children can access collage materials such as wooden 'cookies,' pine-cones, and shells.

TIME TO REFLECT:

Discuss the quote by Grayson Perry as a staff team. What does it mean to you?

Conclusion

To promote good wellbeing, an outdoor space should be set up in response to observations, discussions with children, and co-playing, and it should be flexible enough to evolve in response to the developing needs and interests of the children using it.

Children need a rich, varied outdoor space for their physical and mental wellbeing. They see the outdoor space in terms of what it can offer them, and they need to be able to change and manipulate the space themselves.

Working in early years is a complex role. The priority is to ensure that the play space meets the needs of the children who use it. Try to resist spending extra time creating a space that only meets the approval of adults. Consult the children and find out how they view the space – you may be surprised!

TIME TO REFLECT:

- Are there different gradients in the outdoor space to enable children to improve balance and gross motor skills?
- How could you consult the children at your setting about the design of the outdoor space?
- How is your outdoor space 'zoned'?

References

 Reading for children

Browne, A. (2005). *Into the Forest*. London: Walker Books.

Gravett, E. and Henry, L. (2018). *Tidy*. London: Two Hoots.

Hutchins, H.J., Herbert, G. and Petričić, D. (2008). *Mattland*. Toronto: Annick Press.

Sharratt, N. (2010). *Foggy, Foggy Forest*. London: Walker Books Ltd.

Winslow, M. and Blegvad, E. (2010). *Mud Pies and Other Recipes*. New York: New York Review of Books.

 Reading for adults

Anna Freud Centre. (2020). *Relationships and Belonging*. Mentally Healthy Schools. [online] www.mentallyhealthyschools.org.uk. Available at: https://www.mentallyhealthyschools.org.uk/risks-and-protective-factors/school-based-risk-factors/relationships-and-belonging/.

BBC News. (2007). Dirt exposure "boosts happiness." *news.bbc.co.uk*. [online] 1 April. Available at: http://news.bbc.co.uk/1/hi/health/6509781.stm [Accessed 14 March 2021].

Birch, J., Parnell, R., Patsarika, M. and Šorn, M. (2017). Creativity, play and transgression: Children transforming spatial design. *CoDesign*, 13(4), 245–260. doi:10.1080/15710882.2016.1169300

Birch, J., Parnell, R., Patsarika, M. and Šorn, M. (2017). Participating together: Dialogic space for children and architects in the design process. *Children's Geographies*, 15(2), 224–236. doi:10.1080/14733285.2016.1238039

Bruce, T. (2004). *Time to Play in Early Childhood Education*. London: Hodder & Stoughton.

Conner, T.S., DeYoung, C.G. and Silvia, P.J. (2018). Everyday creative activity as a path to flourishing. *The Journal of Positive Psychology*, 13(2), 181–189. doi:10.1080/17439760.2016.1257049

Heckmann, H. (2016). *Nokken: A Garden for Children: A Danish Approach to Waldorf-Based Child Care*. New York: Waldorf Early Childhood Association North America.

Heft, H. (1988). Affordances of children's environments: A functional approach to environmental description. *Children's Environment Quality*, 29–37.

Jack, G. (2015). I may not know who I am, but I know where I am from: The meaning of place in social work with children and families. *Child and Family Social Work*, 20(4), 415–423.

Lowry, C., et al. (2007). Identification of an immune-responsive mesolimbocortical serotonergic system: Potential role in regulation of emotional behaviour. *Neuroscience*. doi:10.1016/j.neuroscience.2007.01.067

Morgan, P. (2009). Towards a developmental theory of place attachment. *Journal of Environmental Psychology*, 30(1), 11–22.

National Disability Authority. (2018). The 7 principles | Centre for excellence in universal design [online], *Universaldesign.ie*. Available at: http://universaldesign.ie/What-is-Universal-Design/The-7-Principles/.

Nebelong, H. (2002). *Free Play Network*. [online] www.freeplaynetwork.org.uk. Available at: http://www.freeplaynetwork.org.uk/design/nebelong.htm [Accessed 10 February 2021].

Nicholson, S. (1971). How not to cheat children: The theory of loose parts. *Landscape Architecture*, 62, 30–35.

3 | The wellbeing laboratory

Wellbeing themes in this chapter:

Collaboration...Critical thinking...Decision making...
Leadership...Problem solving

Introduction

"What things do you like to play with when you are outside?"
"Trees or things to climb. Ropes. Tools. I just like there to be stuff
like balls and tyres and mud." Jack

My house is 150 years old and was abandoned for years. When the
estate agent showed us round this empty, unloved house, I was dis-
turbed by a small room that was completely tiled, with large vicious
hooks hanging from the ceiling: it reminded me of a horror film setting. However, the estate agent quickly explained that the hooks would
have held cured bacon, rabbits, and pheasants – this was just an old-
fashioned larder.

"The object offers what it does because it is what it is." (Gibson, 1979)

'Affordances' in the environment make an offer to a person or reveal
a possible function (Gibson, 1979), and they are unique and different
for everyone (Kyttä, 2002). A child-friendly environment offers multiple
affordances that children are able to actualise (Kyttä, 2003).

DOI: 10.4324/9781003137023-3

When children enter a play space, they use their senses to explore every aspect (including walls and fences), and they consider how each bit can become part of their play. Because young children are often encountering objects for the very first time, they are less limited by social norms and so a rope

becomes a bridge or a measuring device or a tug-of-war game. A toy car, on the other hand, is recognised for what it is and will simply be pushed along the ground (Education Scotland, 2009). It's true that children sometimes use toys in surprising and enterprising ways, but open-ended objects inspire children to think in more fluid ways – what I like to call possibility thinking. Playing with ideas in this way can reduce anxiety, depression, and stress, and, as we continue to push the boundaries with technology, and experience increasing pressure to solve issues like climate change, we're going to need a society of critical thinkers.

> *"Children are more interested in the box that a fancy toy comes in. The box is everything, and the box can be anything. Too often, we are structuring and shaping everything. We are taking the boxes away from children all the time. Let them have the box." Sharie Coombs, neuropsychotherapist*

What are loose parts?

"I got the sticks, and I made a bridge then I went over it!" Joseph

Loose parts are materials that are open ended, offering multiple play possibilities. A stick, for example, can be a drum beater, a wand, a marker,

a torch, or a potion stirrer. A good range of different types of loose parts is best for emotional development, and this tends to happen quite naturally because loose parts are often picked up for free or donated.

Loose parts in the outdoor space could include:

Plastic crates, cable reels, sections of guttering, buckets, tyres, bicycle wheels, cardboard tubes, wooden planks, wooden blocks, ropes, wooden pallets, flowers, sand, pine cones, shells, leaves, pods, seeds, stones, logs, sticks, twigs, log slices, bark, sand, gravel, hay, ice.

In fact, the list of possibilities is never-ending. Architect Simon Nicholson, who coined the term loose parts, included in his definition: smells, electricity, magnetism, gravity, gases, fluids, sounds, music, motion, chemical interactions, fire, words, concepts, and ideas.

TIME TO REFLECT:

How could loose parts play help children see themselves as more competent?

Historical advocates of loose parts

"Better a broken bone than a broken spirit." Lady Allen Hurtwood

Children have always played with materials that are not specifically toys, but certain key figures have championed loose parts play. One of these is the remarkable Lady Allen of Hurtwood, referred to by author Tim Gill as the 'godmother of play' (Gill, 2013). During World War II, Lady Allen worked on a European initiative to help orphaned and displaced children, and, while her plane was refuelling in Copenhagen, she was taken by the Head of the Froebel Institute in Copenhagen to see a new play space, opened in 1943. This meeting changed not only Lady Allen's life but also outdoor play in the UK (Wilson, n.d.).

The Emdrup Junk Playground, sometimes referred to as the birthplace of playwork, was the very first adventure playground, and enabled children to create on a large scale, with free access to wood, rope, canvas, tyres, wire, bricks, pipes, rocks, logs, balls, wheels, and other loose parts. During the Nazi occupation, antisocial behaviour increased, and play was seen as a way to reinstate a sense of community (Kozlovsky, 2016). Emdrup's creator, Carl Theodor Sorensen, had observed that children preferred to play on bomb sites, and at Emdrup, it was the children who decided what to build or demolish, how to share tools and building materials, and how to resolve disagreements and fights (Kozlovsky, 2016). Sorensen was dedicated to changing public parks from places that simply looked attractive to places where children could play, and he believed that play areas might not look aesthetically pleasing because children don't always play in adult-friendly ways.

Lady Hurtwood was inspired and brought the idea of adventure playgrounds back to the UK, where they became wildly popular with children: "there was a wealth of waste material on it and no man-made fixtures. The children could dig, build houses, experiment with sand, water or fire, and play games of adventure and make-believe" (Wilson, n.d.).

Architect Simon Nicholson, who developed 'The Theory of Loose Parts,' felt that adventure playgrounds were unique because this was where chil-dren could build and shape their environment. Carbon-copy playgrounds, on the other hand, were seen by Nicholson as like prisons: "clean, static and impossible to play around with" (Nicholson, 1971). Nicholson stated that the education system stifled children's natural creativity, and he advocated for a "laboratory type environment where they can experiment, enjoy and find out things for themselves" (Nicholson, 1971).

To Nicholson, loose parts were an essential part of a healthy, stimulating play space and he felt the best way for young children to learn was through discovery, within a rich, possibility-filled environment co-created by children themselves (Nicholson, 1971).

TIME TO REFLECT:

How can we involve children as co-creators of play spaces?

Sourcing loose parts

"I collect them. All the other children … they know I collect them, so they get them for me and put them in my collection." Christopher

Loose parts do need replacing regularly because they are played with so thoroughly. Because I've seen them played with in so many different ways, I get attached to them and feel a sense of loss when I finally have to get rid of a crate or a rope! My pupils are skilled at identifying when something has become too hazardous.

Sourcing outdoor loose parts:

- Buy them from suppliers. (A time-saving option and you can order what you need.)

- Browse charity shops or join a local scrapstore. (Reducing landfill is a great way to protect children's future wellbeing.)

- Ask builders on-site! They are often delighted to get rid of items such as cable reels.

- Use the network of employees/business owners linked to the children at your setting and send home a wish list with the children. (Also a good way to build the relationship with families and the wider community.)

- Host a 'scrap swap' for local settings. Great for networking and you also get your hands on different loose parts. You may have 200 bottle top lids while the setting down the road has metres and metres of plastic tubing – get swapping!

- Find out if you have a local loose parts lending library.
- Use social media. You will often get a good response to requests for materials.
- Grow and harvest your own loose parts. For example, bamboo, flower petals, and herbs stimulate good-quality sensory play. You can also forage for loose parts such as sticks, stones, and pine cones, but only take items from the ground and don't take too many. Be aware of local guidance – you can be prosecuted in some areas for taking stones from beaches.
- Remember to check donations for potential hazards and support the children to thank donors because they will be keen to donate again in the future. Also, expressing gratitude strengthens relationships and being grateful is associated with feelings of increased happiness.

One of the most attractive things about freely available loose parts is that they often reflect the community where the setting is based (Casey and Robertson, 2016), which enhances children's community connection. Hampden Way nursery, for example, has sections of a large London Underground map in the outdoor space. Having discussions about locally sourced loose parts can help children understand what makes their community distinctive. Within my school's community, for example, local farmers employ many migrant workers (whose children attend the school) and the farms donate empty strawberry punnets and boxes. Big employers within a community can have a significant impact on family wellbeing.

Feeling that we belong helps us form healthy relationships (Maslow, 1943), and feeling that we belong to a wider community improves our sense of place. Widening the lens still further, we can help children see that they belong to a global community by showing them examples of loose parts play at other settings across the world – children quickly pick up on the fact that other children play in similar ways.

Revisiting Nicholson's definition of loose parts opens up a whole world of possibilities. Now we are in the realm of creating fire with children or even playing with words or ideas. Remember our child-led audit of the space? What are the names children have for different areas? Be playful with these words. For example, we have "roll hill," "squish path," and *"pirat* tree." (This is a Polish word pronounced 'pee-rat.') You can already see the play potential here! An induction for new children that includes children's names for play places would be meaningful for new starters.

In terms of playing with sounds, take a Bluetooth speaker outside and ask the children to choose the sounds or music they want to accompany their play. One of my pupils, who had made a castle from loose parts, requested 'castle sounds,' and, when this search didn't produce any results, we searched for 'medieval village' sounds. We sat inside his castle together, enthralled by the sound of cart-wheels rattling over cobble stones, the black-smith's hammer striking the anvil, and honking geese being driven to market. We talked about living without electricity or cars or the internet, and his 'castle' then gained a forge for sword making. Try a space soundtrack or the sounds of a waterfall to inspire interesting outdoor play. Conceal a speaker playing rainforest sounds next to branches, leaves, and other natural loose parts and see what happens! Great opportunities for sensory play.

TIME TO REFLECT:

Are there other ways that community connection might enhance wellbeing?

Introducing loose parts

"My best thing is the sand, and I like the sand going through the funnels, two funnels, that funnel then that funnel." Jake

When I brought loose parts into a setting for the first time, I just dumped them in the playground with no explanation, and, as predicted by a sceptical member of staff, many children seemed to be on a mission to break as many as possible. Not my proudest teaching moment, and it felt chaotic and uncomfortable. However, when the children realised the loose parts weren't going to be

taken away and they had uninterrupted time to play with them, everything changed. Within 48 hours the playground was eerily quiet as all children focused on a self-directed challenge, either on their own or with friends. The adult who was initially concerned looked around at the children combining loose parts in different ways and commented that it was the best session she'd ever supervised.

Large outdoor loose parts need to be introduced properly, just as you would with any aspect of continuous provision. In my current setting, loose parts were introduced to the whole school using the services of Scrapstore PlayPod, who can provide training for staff as well as loose parts and storage sheds. They explain rules such as 'scrap on scrap not on people.' It's important to talk through how to use loose parts like ropes, which offer so many options but can have safety implications.

Early years expert Jan White suggests adding loose parts gradually over the year so that children can keep building on embedded experience and knowledge (White, 2014). Children must have easy access to them.

Putting out loose parts as a provocation – e.g. guttering together with small boats – can stimulate children's creativity, especially when in response to observations of children's play. I find that outdoor play behaviours are often stimulated by books we have shared in class. Recently, the children were exhilarated by strong winds that rattled the trees and stole scarves so we read a beautiful non-fiction picture book on weather which then inspired bike streamers and kite-making. The kites led onto making 'wind rockets' which then stimulated class conversations about how spacecraft splash land in the sea, leading to puddle play!

Discussing as a staff which loose parts to combine together can be interesting – using sand, water, or gravel with other loose parts for example. Some settings, especially those with older children, set weekly outdoor loose parts challenges with themes such as ramps, bridges, potions, dens, patterns, collections, colours, home, faces, or reflections. Encouraging children to think of a challenge is great for critical thinking. Different loose parts 'stations' within the play space can also encourage deep engagement. Don't be afraid to adapt loose parts when they are donated, especially if you receive a large amount of the same thing.

However, spending an hour creating an artfully arranged display of loose parts outdoors to look beautiful on social media doesn't support children's wellbeing. It's better to evaluate how children are playing with loose parts and introduce items that could extend their play. Make decisions consciously, reflecting on what you've seen. I use baskets to introduce items that could extend the loose parts play I've seen. For example, after watching a group of children using herbs and dirt to make potions, I placed a basket nearby, filled with plastic bottles, tea strainers, scissors, and lemon juice. This special delivery was seized on with delight.

> *"What did children do with the loose parts? What did they discover or rediscover? What concepts were involved? Did they carry their ideas back into the community and their family? Out of all possible materials that could be provided, which ones were the most fun to play with and the most capable of stimulating the cognitive, social and physical learning processes?" Simon Nicholson (1971)*

When children are exploring their schematic interests, they are involved in play that really engages them, and setting up appropriate provocations based on observations can help their emotional wellbeing. Author Michelle Thornhill has made a table that links easily available loose parts with different schemas, as you can see in the appendix available online. Thornhill emphasises that lines between schemas are not always clearly defined and interest in one schema can quickly grow into interest in another.

TIME TO REFLECT:

How can adults enhance loose parts play?

Challenges

> *"The complaints from parents at the start made me wonder if I'd made the right decision, but the children showed them how much they loved loose parts." Julie, nursery teacher*

Loose parts outdoors are great for social skills and for extending children's thinking, but there are challenges.

Parents and colleagues may have reservations about what they see as 'junk' in the outdoor area, and a friend was once told by his Deputy Head that loose parts "ruined the look of the playground." However, I've found that adults who initially have concerns can sometimes become the best advocates for loose parts play when they see the benefits. It can be useful to book playworkers to run training or liaise with local schools that are further along the loose parts journey.

Storage of loose parts can be an issue, especially if you share the space and have to pack away resources after each play session:

- Consider what can be left out, e.g. logs and tyres can be left out in all weather.
- Share the responsibility for putting away loose parts with the children.
- An organised shed or storage system saves work in the long run. It can be tempting to simply chuck everything in but you will regret it! Children often have specific ideas about what they want to construct, and you can find yourself helping them hunt down den-making clips so…
- …collect containers to keep the space organised and make it easier for children to access different loose parts. I find laundry baskets are brilliant.
- If you have access to a shed, hang a piece of washing line high up inside for storing large pieces of material.
- Have discussions when children are reluctant to dismantle their creations. If there is a pressing need to take it apart, talk this through.

TIME TO REFLECT:

What specific challenges do you face in your setting in terms of large loose parts?

Managing loose parts

Loose parts are there for the children and so children make the best loose parts guardians – this gives them a sense of responsibility and encourages them to make decisions, key to social and emotional learning. We want to encourage children to make their own evaluations and consider con-

sequences. Giving children as much responsibility as they can handle also reduces needlessly destructive play. Manipulating loose parts in different ways helps children understand cause and effect but repeatedly smash-ing a piece of wood against a wall until it breaks is less help-ful to wellbeing (of children and practitioners!). If children under-stand that they are the 'custodians' of the outdoor play materials, they feel trusted, valued, and respected.

The few rules I have around loose parts play were devised together with the children and they understand the reasons behind them. Sometimes, specific guidance might be created during a play session, and much of the time, it's about protecting the wellbeing of others. For example, this week I heard one child say to another: "can you move your crates over there? The tower is crashing in the sandpit and I can't move the sandpit, the sandpit is too heavy!" Here is common sense and effective negotiation!

Sensible rules that prevent harm help children feel included and loved. If one of my pupils is moving a large stick in my setting, others will quickly remind him/her to drag it or move it like a walking stick. As I watched a group of children roll a large cable reel slowly and carefully over an enthusiastic child, lying on the ground between the tracks of the wheel, I heard one of the children repeatedly asking: "Do you feel safe?!" The child on the floor confirmed that he did feel safe and sprang up with excitement after their plan worked! Sometimes accidents do hap-pen. One of my pupils recently managed to slightly injure his friend with a stone and he was inconsolable. He needed much more comforting than his friend who eventually said to him: "look, I'm fine and you've learned a lesson!"

When we say 'yes' more to different types of loose parts play, children can develop critical thinking skills, which in turn have been shown to pro-mote wellness in later life (Butler, 2012).

We can support critical thinking by:

- Encouraging curiosity.
- Making available a wide range of loose parts.
- Avoiding intervening unless necessary and giving children sufficient time to try things out.
- Engaging rather than simply responding with a conversation stopper.
- Avoiding talking just for the sake of talking or talking *for* a child.
- Using sustained shared thinking to develop a child's train of thought together.
- Encouraging children to go beyond giving the answer they think we want to hear. Engineers working together on a project may disagree but they give reasons why.
- Encouraging children to make predictions: "What do you think will happen when you do that?"
- Allowing some manageable frustration and struggle.
- Modelling critical thinking processes out loud ourselves.

TIME TO REFLECT:

How do you judge when to intervene in outdoor loose parts play?

In the next section, we look at a Canadian loose parts study and find out about the work of a loose parts company based in Berlin.

The Physical Literacy in the Early Years (PLEY) project, Nova Scotia

Through this scheme, pre-school settings were given a loose parts pack, including buckets, tree cookies, balls, a tarpaulin, tubing, and crates, for a six-month period. The project was led by Professor Michelle Stone: "ultimately, our interests are focused on healthier, happier, more resilient children. We are helping to unlock the power of play" (PLEY, 2019).

The benefits of the project were grouped into five areas:

Risk taking

Educators involved in the study found that loose parts play outdoors helped children become less fearful and able to take progressively more healthy risks. Children were better able to understand their own capabilities and capacities, and their perseverance improved. The educators also changed their attitudes and language: "you're just so used to saying, 'oh be careful, be careful, be careful, don't do that.'" Educators became confident about taking a step back: "I realized they don't need me, I'm just going to sit back and keep my eye on them, and now I just let them go ... they really don't need me right there."

Creativity and imagination

The children were more absorbed and used the loose parts in ways the educators could not have predicted. One educator commented: "they take adventures every day." I find it joyful accompanying children on these adventures. For example, seeing whether it's possible to catch rain in a pan and transport it via a drainpipe to an old bird's nest "because the chicks are thirsty!"

Determination and resilience

As Piaget said, "play is the work of childhood," and the study found the children were absolutely committed to achieving the goals they had set themselves: "they're more determined to see it through to the end than if they were in the classroom." The children showed less frustration and increased perseverance in problem solving, and the adults shared the children's sense of exhilaration when they succeeded.

Independence and confidence

Children grew in confidence and self-esteem and didn't want help or need direction from adults. Shy and introverted children became more self-assured, and one child, who was generally quiet, felt immense pride in his invention when all the other children lined up to see it.

Relationship and leadership

Educators found that loose parts play encouraged children to work together and cooperate. Children partnered up together to achieve goals and literally cheered each other on. There were high levels of engagement and less conflict: "because they've built it together, they don't try to, you know, push each other off or jump in front of each other as much." New friendships were formed, and some older children took on a mentoring role. "It was really nice to see how they worked together and were mentoring each other and cooperating and helping the younger ones" (PLEY, 2019).

From Nova Scotia, let's go to Berlin!

CASE STUDY: SOLUTION-ORIENTED ACTION

Bewegungsbaustelle.berlin offers loose parts sessions for children aged 18 months and over, and is run by Henning Camin and Martin Stief. Henning comments: "we do our Bewegungsbaustelle outside because we want the kids to be in the fresh air. In our area of Berlin, the kids are in small kindergartens, and they don't have proper room for sports."

Henning avoids having loose parts that match together in sets because the aim is for the children to use their imagination to combine the materials, rather than being able to simply fit them together like Lego blocks. "Children have this imagination inside and they need the freedom of play to create their own things. This makes them self-confident and it makes them aware of their own skills. BBS is not a finished 'end product.'"

Independence is encouraged: "I don't tell the kids what to do, I don't help them solve problems, I don't help them lift something or build something. I want them to act on their own to realise what they are capable of." The children devise their own plans and negotiate to share the materials, a process which BBS calls 'solution-oriented action.' This process requires high-quality language and social interaction – sometimes the children have to stand up for themselves, confront other children, or use persuasion. Communication skills are also improved through role play, which Henning finds happens naturally.

Henning comments: "the kids develop social skills and cognitive skills and also motor skills through walking, jumping, climbing and balancing. Bewegungsbaustelle gives kids the opportunity to realise themselves. They learn in an environment that is about feeling and exploring knowledge."

Tips from BBS:

- Invest in good storage.
- Include an interesting variety of materials to keep children interested.
- Pay full attention to children throughout their play.
- Allow free play but talk about how to handle the materials and establish the rules. Clarity and transparency are the basis of self-regulation.
- Less adult input is more. The children need freedom so that they can develop their own creative ideas.
- Give advice when there is conflict but avoid being an arbitrator. Conflicts are valuable and children need to learn to resolve conflicts on their own. Have discussions: rule conflicts are good conversations to have.
- Do not intervene prematurely. This applies both to construction issues and to risk situations.

- Explain that one group cannot take over another group's constructions.
- Let children play a major role in setting up, playing, and dismantling.

Loose parts play for emotional competence

Here are some observations from my setting during one play session that illustrate how loose parts play can support emotional wellbeing.

Lexie

Following relentless rain, the ground was treacherously muddy. As the children's feet slid, they adjusted their steps accordingly, putting their arms out to balance. Lexie laboriously dragged a small cable reel next to a larger one, and, gripping the far end of the small cable reel, she pulled the rest of her body onto it and then stepped onto the larger reel. Without hesitation, she launched herself into the air. I was instantly alert. She landed on her feet but unbalanced and ended up on her hands and knees in the mud, giggling.

Without a word, three other children came over and started to copy Lexie. Here, you could see leadership and also a child who is beginning to anticipate the consequences of her actions and evaluate them. Lexie decided not to jump so far next time and stretched her arms out. This time she stayed on her feet when she landed. Solution-oriented thinking! When Lexie's peers reached the highest cable reel, they were more apprehensive. One child needed me to hold her hand while she jumped. Another hesitated and nervously shuffled backwards. Others quickly stepped in to offer a hand to hold. He was anxious and, at the last minute, he simply let himself go and fell. He was tearful but decided to try again ... and again. I had to stop myself from stepping in and 'rescuing' him, allowing him to persevere and discover his own capacities. Afterwards, we talked through the process together, discussing how he'd felt and what an achievement it had been to keep going when things got difficult and painful (emotionally and physically!).

Freddie and Grace

The two children pulled a large piece of material over a tuff spot on a stand and climbed inside. Freddie pulled two phone headsets into the den so that they were dangling above their heads by the cords. They laughed excitedly and whispered to each other. Three other children suddenly burst into the den, dislodging the material. Grace and Freddie were visibly annoyed and told the interlopers to leave, and one did, pulling the material back over the top. I couldn't make out the spoken words, but the remaining children persuaded Grace and Freddie that they should be able to stay. All children then began to talk on the phone handsets.

If I had stepped in to sort things out for them, they would not have worked to find the right words to state their case. There can be frustration when you try to get your point across to someone with an opposing view but choosing words to confront, negotiate, and heal, without resorting to physicality, is a significant display of social and emotional competence.

Grace then informed the group that the den needed an extra room. She told everyone to listen and gave each child a task. Another tuff spot on a stand was pulled over and a large piece of material was thrown over the top and pulled into place. There was some discussion about whether the material should divide the two 'rooms' in half. Grace decided that the two rooms should be 'together.' The children now had a private child-governed space away from adult surveillance.

In this case, loose parts encouraged discussion and negotiation, and the children had to deal with strong emotions, including frustration and resentment. Some children had to put themselves in another's shoes and use persuasion to remain involved and part of the group. A clear leader emerged and took charge, and brought the children together as a team, focused on one goal.

Cerys

Cerys sat on the ground next to the fence amongst wind-blown fallen leaves. She didn't seem to notice the wet ground and was utterly absorbed by examining the leaves, turning them over. Her engagement was clear. When she noticed I was taking photos, she turned and smiled, but then became re-engaged by her activity.

Cerys felt safe and secure enough to dedicate all her attention to her chosen task for around 45 minutes. It seemed to be a mindful task that relaxed her busy thoughts and restored her concentration and attention. Csikszentmihalyi talks about flow being 'autotelic': "the key element of an optimal experience is that it is an end in itself. Even if initially undertaken for other reasons, the activity that consumes us becomes intrinsically rewarding" (Csikszentmihalyi, 1991). He also points out that formal education can sometimes hinder experience of flow. Do we allow enough time for children to become fully and actively involved in an absorbing self-directed activity? Do we move at their pace or do we encourage them to move at ours?

Bartek

Movement is said to be the first language of children, and physical activity is great for building vocabulary and confidence. Getting the children to make an obstacle course using loose parts, for example, is fantastic for language and collaboration. The children tour around each other's sections following their peers' instructions: "walk across the plank, then jump into the tyre, then crawl under the tarpaulin." Research shows that children learn motion verbs more quickly when they perform the actions themselves, and outdoors there are many more opportunities for children to be hands-on.

Children tend to feel most comfortable and least worried about 'getting it wrong' outdoors. Bartek, who mainly speaks Polish, was playing outside on the lid of a large wooden sandpit, with an English-speaking boy. Bartek repeatedly jumped off the sandpit, shouting a sentence in Polish. His friend caught the word: "Batman" in the sentence, and they both began to jump off, shouting: "Batman!" They started to exchange words with each other, and, through a mixture of miming and English and Polish words, they decided on their characters. During their role play, the English speaker said "Batmobile" to Bartek then "car," using a small tyre as a steering wheel. "Car" Bartek repeated, mimicking the steering wheel motion. They both zoomed off, driving their hero vehicles. The boys showed empathy and were able to solve the communication issue together.

> *"By incorporating lots of hands on, independent learning experiences, children learning English can participate without the need for fluent English. As can be seen here, the children were learning through play without even realising it. This immersive approach should lead to rapid progress and it is quite normal for children in early years to code switch between languages as they learn – sometimes even within the same sentence!" Beth Southern, founder of the EAL Hub*

What comes through strongly in each play example is that loose parts enable children to be decision makers, designing, analysing, evaluating, and reflecting. Loose parts are inclusive, allowing children to participate in the way that they choose.

Conclusion

A loose parts laboratory enables children to take the initiative and carry out hands-on problem solving. There's no right or wrong approach, and children become confident to try things out and use critical thinking.

Introducing loose parts to the outdoor space can improve behaviour and engagement, making it a much better experience for adults and children. Children learn that people have different perspectives and develop empathy and conflict resolution skills.

TIME TO REFLECT:

- How do you ensure that the children in your setting have access to a wide range of loose parts?
- Is your storage of loose parts easily accessible to children?
- Are there aspects of loose parts play that you feel require more adult guidance?

References

Reading for children

Portis, A. (2009). *Not a Stick*. New York: HarperCollins.
Portis, A. (2014). *Not a Box*. New York: Harper 360.

Reading for adults

Allen, M. and Nicholson, M. (1975). *Memoirs of an Uneducated Lady: Lady Allen of Hurtwood.* London: Thames and Hudson.

Butler, H. (2012). Halpern critical thinking assessment predicts real-world outcomes of critical thinking. *Applied Cognitive Psychology,* 26(5). doi:10.1002/acp.2851

Casey, T. and Robertson, J. (2016). *Loose Parts Play, a Toolkit.* [online]. Available at: https://www.inspiringscotland.org.uk/wp-content/up loads/2017/03/Loose-Parts-Play-web.pdf.

Csikszentmihalyi, M. (1991). *Flow: The Psychology of Optimal Experience.* San Francisco: Harper Perennial.

Education Scotland, 2009. *Outdoor Learning: Practical Guidance, Ideas and Support for Teachers and Practitioners in Scotland.* Livingston, Education Scotland.

Gibson, J.J. (1979). *The Ecological Approach to Visual Perception.* Boston: Houghton Mifflin.

Gill, T. (2013). Lady Allen – The godmother of play – Speaks. [online] *Rethinking Childhood.* Available at: https://rethinkingchildhood.co m/2013/06/24/lady-allen-godmother-play/.

Kozlovsky, R. (2016). Princeton University School of Architecture. Paper presented at *The Threat and Youth Conference,* Teachers College (1 April, 2006).

Kyttä, M. (2002). Affordances of children's environments in the context of cities, small towns, suburbs and rural villages in Finland and Belarus. *Journal of Environmental Psychology,* 22(1–2), 109–123. doi:10.1006/jevp.2001.0249

Kyttä, M. (2003). *CHILDREN IN OUTDOOR CONTEXTS Affordances and Independent Mobility in the Assessment of Environmental Child Friendliness.* Helsinki: Helsinki University of Technology, A Centre for Urban and Regional Studies.

Maslow, A.H. (1943). A theory of human motivation. *Psychological Review,* 50(4), 370–396.

PLEY (Physical Literacy in the Early Years). (2019). *Evaluation Report.* Halifax: Dalhousie University.

Nicholson, S. (1971). How NOT to cheat children – The theory of loose parts, *Landscape Architecture*, 62, 30–34.

White, J. (2014). *Being, Playing and Learning Outdoors: Making Provision for High Quality Experiences in the Outdoor Environment with Children 3–7.* New York: Routledge.

Wilson, P. (n.d.). "Children are more complicated than kettles." The life and work of Lady Allen of Hurtwood. – *Penny Wilson.* [online] theinternationale.com. Available at: http://theinternationale.com/pennywilson/38-2/.

Dare to play

Wellbeing themes in this chapter:

Autonomy...Competence...Freedom...Independence...
Perseverance...Responsibility

"If I get scared, I still want to try it, so I do it, and then I do it again and again and again until I can do it. Easy." Jack

Introduction

"I feel like I want to try, but if my friends do it too, I feel braver. If someone shows me first, I'm not scared as much, and I want to try it more." Edie

DOI: 10.4324/9781003137023-4

"Avoiding danger is no safer in the long run than outright exposure ... life is either a daring adventure or nothing." (Helen Keller, 1946)

Dr Judith Klein, an assistant professor of emergency medicine, defines play with risk as "child directed play which allows the child to recognise and evaluate a challenge and decide upon a course of action" (Klein, 2016). This type of 'daring' play can sometimes be uncomfortable for adults, and at times, we may need to talk about the benefits with parents and colleagues. The dictionary definition of 'daring' is to be adventurous or audaciously bold, causing outrage or surprise – adventurous play can be unsettling for observers. However, "children know what they need for their bodies and their senses" (Klein, 2016).

Kathryn Solly, who has written extensively on the concept of play with risk, refers to the process of moving into the 'stretch zone' (Solly, 2015), and if you watch young children playing outdoors, you see them continually striving to test their capacities. Children instinctively want to push the boundaries, explore hidden spaces, and build their knowledge of the world around them. When children choose to play adventurously, they choose to be curious and daring, and, as Edie states above, they need the encouragement of their peers, and they also need us.

TIME TO REFLECT:

How do you feel about adventurous play?

Equity and inclusivity

Taking a risk in play is not always about physical risk. 'April' still recalls her teacher firmly steering her away from the sparkly pink dresses and jewellery in the class dressing-up box. Assigned male at birth, she always knew she was a girl. The bias shown by April's teacher created further confusion and anxiety, so that playing in the way she wanted to became risky. Even if we are not consciously aware of it, we express our attitudes and values through our provision and our language – the 'hidden curriculum' (Vasilena Vasileva, 2018). Back in 1902, sociologist Charles Horton Cooley suggested that people tend to base their sense of identity on other people's reactions and perceptions of them (Cooley, 2017), and a child's developing identity is heavily influenced by how others see them. Labels stick, and we need to be aware of prejudice we might have, whether conscious or unconscious.

Inclusivity means ensuring that all feel included, and for this to happen, we need to know every child, and challenge discriminatory approaches that limit children in play or push them into risk before they are ready.

> *"When we talk about play, we need to think about the myth of misbehaviour for black boys, and the over policing of the black child and the restricting of play. Black boys are policed in the nursery environment, the school environment and within wider society.*
>
> *T'ziyah was a boy who came to me after being excluded from three different day nurseries but when he came to me, he was a delight. He was articulate and enjoyable to be around. This was a four-year-old boy who had already been told: 'You're naughty, you don't belong here.'*
>
> *Risky play is important and outdoor play can be where the magic happens, especially for black boys. They can do all the things they have been told they can't do inside: 'don't run, don't fidget.' Outdoor play for black boys can be freedom."* Liz Pemberton, the Black Nursery Manager

It's our responsibility to make sure all children can fully participate in outdoor play, and providing equitable play opportunities means recognising that we're all different and need varying levels of support. Children with special educational needs are often unnecessarily restricted from taking part in adventurous play (Caprino, 2018), and the social model of disability, developed by disabled people, proposes that people are disabled by physical or attitudinal barriers in society, not by their impairment. When we remove these barriers, it opens up more independence, choice, and control (Shakespeare, 2004).

We also need to be aware of our unconscious bias in terms of gender. In one study, the emotional reactions of parents were very different according to the gender of the child: boys' risk-taking elicited anger and disciplinary reactions, whereas responses to the same risk-taking by girls were focused around safety, and parents expressed disappointment and surprise (Morrongiello et

al., 2010). Sometimes, we have to work against unhelpful beliefs that children have internalised.

"Schools with an inclusive orientation are the most effective means of combating discriminatory attitudes, creating welcoming communities, building an inclusive society and achieving education for all." (Gareth Moorewood, 2014)

TIME TO REFLECT:

Do you have regular discussions with colleagues on inclusivity and equity?

Barriers to adventurous play

"If children are given freedom to explore their surroundings, they are able to stretch their capabilities and will learn what risks they can take, or how far they can push themselves. Too often, it is the adult's fear being transferred to the children which limits them and restricts their imagination." Anne MacAskill (mother of Danny MacAskill, street trials rider)

In recent years, official bodies such as the Health and Safety Executive (HSE) have encouraged a more balanced approach to adventurous play, making it clear that the perceived fear of litigation and prosecution has been blown out of proportion. However, some settings are still reluctant to enable children to take appropriate risk in their play.

"It used to be the staff preventing children ... well me really. Wanting to keep them contained, controlled." Reception teacher

Talking to practitioners at different settings highlighted that staffing and the restrictive attitude of some colleagues, leaders, and parents are significant barriers. Adventurous play requires us to be attentive, and if 1 adult is supervising 30 4-year-old children, it's impossible to give them the attention they need. The attitude of other adults can also be limiting. A childminder friend recently asked a parent to take down a social media post detailing her angry complaint about clothes ripped during outdoor play. The parent refused, and the post quickly gained momentum. The 'culture of fear,' as described by Professor Frank Furedi, means that perceptions of risk and safety are often not based on a reasoned evaluation of all the available evidence – people follow cultural norms when deciding what they ought to fear and how they should fear it (Furedi, 1997). So, someone posts online that they are furious their child was 'endangered' during outdoor play and others validate this fear. It's not surprising that parental complaints cause some settings to limit adventurous play. Strong relationships with parents are key, and this is explored in detail in Chapter 6.

Risk assessment

"If you have high expectations, the children will meet them. If you trust them and believe in them and let them have that responsibility, they will live up to that." Lisa Atkinson, Reception teacher

Keeping children safe is not about complicated assessment methods, according to the Health and Safety Executive, and it's not about completely eliminating risk. Sensible judgements need to be used (Children's Play and Leisure). Author and consultant Tim Gill, along with Professor David Ball and Bernard Spiegal, have created a risk-benefit approach which starts with identifying the benefits of the activity and then moves onto considering the potential risks and reviewing the possible responses to these risks before reaching a judgement. A risk-benefit approach is about taking into account the risks whilst recognising the benefits of challenging play experiences, an approach which is supported by the HSE. Establishing a balance where children are able to take healthy risks in their play without being in unnecessary danger is the best possible outcome for their wellbeing. There are some excellent worked examples of risk-benefit assessment forms online that are free to download.

Dynamic risk assessment is what we do all the time! It's about making on the spot decisions about risk as the outdoor play happens. Chris Holland, storyteller and author, uses an Opportunities, Risks, and Benefits (ORBs) model in response to 'eek moments' such as a child falling over in a slippery, muddy area. The flow chart below explains the process.

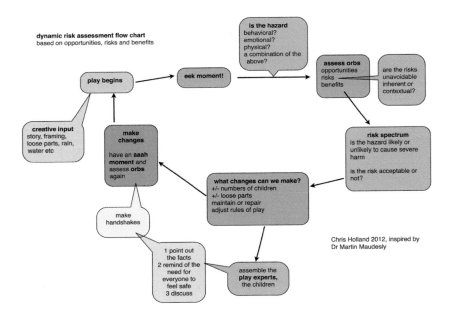

It's important to distinguish between risks and hazards.

- A *hazard* is something that can cause harm.
- A *risk* is the chance, high or low, that any hazard will actually cause somebody harm.

Do we need to remove all hazards from a play environment? A friend who teaches Reception in Portugal grows chillies in the school garden. She has explained to the children that touching the chillies and then touching their eyes will result in intense pain, and this has been a sufficient deterrent. They don't touch the chillies! If children are involved in managing risk, they are much less likely to come to harm.

Supporting children's unstructured outdoor play can be a journey: I've become more confident about trusting children's instincts. However, practitioners need to be honest about any areas of play that make them uncomfortable.

"All our staff believe in allowing risk, and it shines through. When students come in on placement, they are sometimes a little taken aback, but by the time they leave us, they completely understand and get it. It's a good idea to start small until staff are confident." Janine Medway-Smith, Nursery teacher

TIME TO REFLECT:

Are there ways you could further support children to assess risk themselves?

Trust and high expectations

"When I climb trees, daddy checks I'm OK. He asks me if I feel safe and I say 'yes.'" Jenny

When children are supported to assess and manage their own risk, they build their capacity for decision making and problem solving. As well as involving children in the overall risk assessment of the outside area, we can help them to become dynamic risk assessors. For example, a child in my setting began to swing a rope in a wide circle, narrowly missing other children. Another child suggested he should swing it lower, maybe on the ground, because other children looked scared. Someone might get hurt, she said. Young children are capable of thinking analytically about how best to keep themselves and others safe, and, when given responsibility, they can identify potential problems and consider what needs to change (if anything). They judge by facial expressions, movement, and language whether others feel unsafe. Some children need additional support to assess risk, but children don't generally want to injure themselves or others.

If we always step in when things get risky, children get into the habit of turning to the adult for a decision and they doubt their abilities, putting themselves in a vulnerable position when they encounter other challenging situations. Using language that builds confident decision making is more effective.

If a child becomes anxious or 'stuck':

- Don't pressurise them.
- Let them know that you are there to help if needed.
- Listen carefully and read the child's body language.
- Acknowledge and validate the child's feelings.
- Ask open-ended questions such as "how do you feel?" (You may want to link this to physical sensations – "how do you feel in your tummy?")
- If necessary, discuss how the challenge could be made more accessible.
- Celebrate what the child has achieved so far.
- Calmly support the child to talk through the next steps. A big part of emotional intelligence is being able to 'self-instruct.'
- Ask another child to model it so that you can watch and discuss together.
- If the child changes their mind, reassure them that that's OK.

I once worked in a setting where the photocopier was ferociously guarded. If exact protocol was not used, I would hear a loudly shouted: "STOP!" prompting me to drop all the paper on the floor! I've seen a similar thing happen in some playgrounds. It's not helpful for emotional wellbeing.

It also doesn't help if we show that we, as adults, are fearful and unsettled. My son once sustained a serious concussion at school, caused by a football stud to the head. The junior doctor on duty at the hospital examined my 6-ft teen, babbling, vomiting, and rolling his eyes. The panic showed on her face. "I'm really very worried about him," she nervously exclaimed, and fear struck my heart like a dagger. At that moment, I needed her to mask her anxiety and instil calm in me by remaining calm herself.

TIME TO REFLECT:

If we encourage children to take a risk if they are not ready, what could the impact be?

Observing play with risk

"I saw it when I was jumping off! I watched it again and again with mummy on the computer." Alex

Watching children's play helps us judge the level of support they need, rather than restricting play unnecessarily, or forcing children to risk more than they want to. It takes time to build trusting relationships, and we need to feel that we have enough time to understand how each child challenges themselves in different contexts. It can be helpful to review how different areas of the outdoor space help children challenge themselves, and if an area is not working, talk with the children about what would work better.

Discussing observations with parents, staff, and the children themselves builds a good understanding of what a child can do and how they want to challenge themselves. Seeing examples of adventurous play outside school has sometimes challenged my assumptions about a child's capabilities.

When I'm observing play that involves risk, I often find I need to put my iPad down (yes, the case is muddy!) and be present. The child needs me to be in the moment, calm and supportive, but also focused. As they achieve something that thrills and frightens them, I get to share their sense of exhilaration (even if my heart is in my mouth!).

Through our interactions with children, we learn what they perceive as taking a risk in play. Watching a group of children recently who had discovered a ladybird, I saw one child circling the group, bobbing his head towards the clustered children but then hastily stepping back. Twenty minutes later, he had built up the confidence to let the ladybird walk on his hand, and he beamed with pride.

Daring play and emotional regulation

Adventurous play can stimulate many emotions, ranging from pleasure to fear, and young children are at an important stage where they are just starting to recognise, express, and understand their emotions. Most children seek out play that provides that 'tickle in the tummy' moment where they are not sure what the consequences will be (Sandseter, 2010). Some years ago, I visited the fortified town of Cittadella in Italy with my husband and children. We walked along the 50 ft high wall surrounding the town and frequently stopped to admire the jaw-dropping views. Suddenly,

my husband shouted: "DON'T!" He had sensed that our eldest son was considering jumping from the wall to a tree branch – a death-defying leap. Years later, my son still insists he could have landed the jump, and we still insist that he couldn't!

Experiencing strong emotions and discussing them helps children cope with difficult times. I recently coached a child who had climbed up some netting and was terrified about getting back down. "I need help," she said, "I'm too scared." She clung to the netting in fear, but with reassurance and calming discussion, she was able to move her hands and feet to get herself to the bottom. When she saw photographs of this later, she exclaimed: "I was scared." She then added: "but then I could do it!"

Dr Helen Dodd proposes that adventurous play provides important opportunities for children to learn about uncertainty, fear, arousal, and coping. When they have repeated opportunities to explore age-appropriate, healthy risk-taking, children become better prepared to deal with subsequent anxiety and fear-provoking situations (Dodd and Lester, 2021). According to Dodd, exposure to experiences that children are frightened of, such as heights, can actually alleviate that fear,

and even watching other children tackle these challenges can help (Dodd and Lester, 2021). Anxiety has become a significant problem for today's children, and if they are not able to safely practise their responses to fearful situations, the fear can overwhelm.

Dr Klein comments:

> Young children have natural and appropriate fears based upon their abilities and, as they expose themselves to risk, they outgrow these fears. Without risky play, children may never develop this ability to cope with and overcome their fears and may develop extreme risk aversion and anxiety. Early and ample risky play opportunities lead to better impulse control.
>
> (Klein, 2016)

One of my favourite parts of residentials with older children is the moment when they experience fear about an activity but trust in their own capabilities and let go. Talking about it back at school weeks later, children clearly recall the exhilaration and joy at having achieved what they felt was impossible. As adults, we too can experience this rush of dopamine when we remain open to new experiences.

TIME TO REFLECT:

How closely is trust tied up with the act of 'letting go' in adventurous play?

Daring play and perseverance

"Children are often absorbed in their inner world during play. It's about working out who you are, where you are and how to overcome things that stand in your way. That's life, isn't it? It's about mastery and survival. To them, playing is their reality." Sharie Coombes, neuropsychotherapist

Within this play reality, children want to try again and again until they get it. The process of 'failing,' adjusting, and trying again builds physical and emotional resilience. My climber friend, Tom, visualises how he will feel at the top when he is daunted by a new route, and this is a strategy I use with children. How will it feel to achieve this challenge? We can help children respond positively to setbacks by encouraging perseverance:

- Don't swoop in as a rescuer straight away.
- Talk about a relatable challenge that you found difficult and discuss how that felt.
- Use positive language about perseverance: it's OK to 'fail' and try again.
- Praise persistence and focus on the process not the outcome.

With encouragement, children will gladly 'fail' over and over again. I clearly

recall the process of learning to ride a bike: falling off, getting back on, trying again, and I also remember the adult encouraging me.

Minor injuries such as bruises and scratches are part of this process. One of my best birthday gifts as a child was a set of stilts made by my dad. I desperately wanted to be able to take a few steps unaided, and I persevered, making minor adjustments to the position of my hands and feet and the length of my stride. Then one day I fell off the stilts and ended up in hospital. There was no lasting damage, and the main thing I remember is my sense of pride at eventually being able to complete a very wobbly lap of the garden. Children are constantly testing their physical and emotional limits, and play provides the perfect mechanism. If we don't enable this process, we risk creating a society of individuals who lack self-reliance.

This week I watched a child gingerly step onto a vulnerable-looking loose parts construction. He leaned forward to put more weight on his front foot then changed his mind and started to crawl across. By experiencing uncertainty and an appropriate level of risk, children realise that they can (and should) make their own judgements.

TIME TO REFLECT:

How do children develop tenacity and determination?

Sandseter's categories of risky play

"I don't like it when I have to stay inside when it is too windy. I know why, though, I don't want to fly away and land in the queen's garden."
Zayden, who lives in Windsor

To consider why and how children take part in adventurous play and assess what a particular outdoor environment offers to children, it's helpful to explore the categories established by Dr Ellen Sandseter, which you can find in Table 4.1. Dr Sandseter identified and

Table 4.1 Sandseter's categories of risky play

Category	Risk	Subcategories
Great heights.	Danger of injury from falling.	Climbing, jumping from still or flexible surfaces, balancing on high objects, hanging, and swinging at great heights.
High speed.	Uncontrolled speed and pace that can lead to collision with something or someone.	Swinging at high speed, sliding, and sledging at high speed, running uncontrollably at high speed, bicycling at high speed, skating, and skiing at high speed.
Dangerous tools.	Can lead to injuries and wounds.	Cutting tools: knives, saws, axes. Strangling tools: ropes, etc.
Dangerous elements.	Where children can fall into or from something.	Cliffs, deep or icy water, fire pits.
Rough-and-tumble.	Where the children can harm each other.	Wrestling, fencing with sticks, etc. Play fighting.
Disappear/get lost.	Where the children can disappear from the supervision of adults, get lost alone.	Go exploring alone. Playing alone in unfamiliar environments.

categorised these physical risky play characteristics through observation of play at Norwegian pre-schools and interviews at these settings (Sandseter, 2010).

TIME TO REFLECT:

What is your view on climbing, using tools, and rough-and-tumble?

Climbing

As play expert Dr Joe Frost said, "children attempt to scale any object in range" (Frost, 2013). Children instinctively want to climb, and often seek the

highest point they can access. Even babies have climbing skills – how those skills develop depends very much on whether children get the opportunity to practise (Frost, 2013). Climbing requires high levels of concentration and can lead to a state of flow, where stress and anxiety are reduced.

Climbing tips from my friend, Tom:

- Start off on low heights until children are confident.
- Practice – every climbing opportunity helps children learn more about body awareness and balance.
- Reassure children that it's natural to feel apprehensive. Feeling a little bit scared helps us make better decisions.
- Climbers are constantly thinking about their footwork. Encourage children to think about where they are going to place their feet.

Climbing often leads to jumping, and assessing heights and learning to land safely are important skills. I was donated a crash mat by a climber parent, and this has proved useful, especially for young children jumping from loose parts.

"To climb a tree is for a child to discover a new world." Friedrich Froebel, The Education of Man, *1826*

Tree climbing can be a controversial topic, and practitioners need to decide what they are comfortable with. Children in my setting can climb trees when an adult is there to supervise, and it elicits feelings of frustration, determination, anxiety, pride, and exhilaration – all healthy emotions for wellbeing and resilience. One of the hardest parts of tree climbing for children is getting back down again. This can be 'get me down' territory!

Suddenly the child is looking down and it becomes more frightening. Children may need coaching as they co-ordinate their hands and feet. Then, when they become confident climbers, they are able to coach others.

Tools

Children love the responsibility of real tools, and mastering the use of saws, mallets, and drills enhances their belief in their own competence. Getting hands on is the best way for children to learn, and I'm always gratified by children's intense concentration and high levels of engagement.  Risk assessment is obviously essential, and children need to be involved in this process. I find that children usually learn how to use outdoor tools more quickly than classroom tools such as scissors, and they treat tools with respect because we model this.

I often support children to use an old hand drill that my dad gave me. It's a pleasing piece of equipment to use, and it's deeply satisfying to see the spirals of wood appear as the hole is formed. Nevertheless, it is a tool that demands respect, steady hands, and concentration, and using this old drill demands that we are present and in the moment. All other issues or problems are forgotten as the child holds the drill straight and watches carefully to ensure that the hole is true and that the drill bit is not about to slip. There are so many benefits to using tools, including improving fine motor skills and boosting self-confidence, but above all, there is value in simply spending one-to-one time with a child, supporting them to shape their own environment in a small but significant way.

Rough-and-tumble

We need to allow space for a range of different types of play, and rough-and-tumble play has been shown to help children learn self-control and test their own abilities. It is generally boys that enjoy this type of play, but when boys and girls engage in this play together, the play is more complex, with more language involved (Jarvis, 2006).

Of course, the danger is that children will get hurt, but research shows that rough-and-tumble play only leads to fighting 1% of the time (Scott, Panksepp, 2003). At the end of the day, you have to decide what you are comfortable with and communicate that clearly to the children. Here are some of the elements which differentiate rough-and-tumble play from aggression:

- Children smile and laugh.
- Facial expressions are relaxed.
- They are willing participants.
- They come back to the play again and again.
- They may let the other win.
- Children alternate roles (Carlson, 2009).

I find it's pretty straightforward to establish whether children involved in rough-and-tumble play are willing participants. When this is not the case, there is a good opportunity for discussion around the rights of all children in the outside area to feel safe. Rough play can be a way for children to communicate that they are anxious or overwhelmed by their feelings and that they need extra love and care.

Weapon play

When my own children were little, I allowed them to play with a toy bow and arrow, but I banned guns of any kind. They very quickly pointed about the hypocrisy of this rule! I changed my mind, although it did sometimes disturb me to see them pointing toy guns at each other.

Young children don't understand that death is permanent, and weapon play can be an important route for children to process their thoughts and feelings. While working on a kibbutz, I saw lots of pretend 'gun play,' which seemed very natural, as all adults carried guns, mostly machine guns. Weapon play is frequently seen in schools close to military camps, as children role play the job of a loved parent or carer.

Studies show that the social and emotional benefits of weapon play include social bonding, especially among boys (Holland, 2008). However, when I conducted an informal poll on this subject, it became clear that it remains a controversial topic:

"Not banned for me! It's the children's interest so I wouldn't curb that."

"I tell them to pack it in, inevitably going to lead to rough play."

"It was banned at the school I first taught in years ago but I did a piece of action research and changed our policy on this."

"I teach a child who, since the age of 3, has stalked the playground holding sticks like a sniper with an assault rifle. He takes silent, deliberate 'shots' at children and staff. It's hauntingly realistic and worries me to watch."

"Not banned. Why remove the only tools children have to process all that they see and hear on the news, to experiment with power and control, subservience and cruelty etc all in the safety of the play frame."

"I point out to my boys that it's violent to point a gun and pretend to shoot someone. If a child pretended to stab their peer, we would be horrified."

"Pointless banning it, it's natural child development and they still do it anyway but casually pretend it's a camera/water pistol if someone looks their way!"

"I don't allow it because weapons are only designed to cause harm to others."

"Not banned. Children have a defence mechanism for handling fear – they use symbolic weapons for good defeating evil and explore their fears in a safe environment. Self-protection as well as a good outlet for emotions."

As adults, we are rightly apprehensive about weapons because of their capacity to maim and kill. We understand the permanence of death. However, if we consider a child's thinking during weapon play, are they not simply thinking in the same way as we do in paintballing? When I'm shooting at my friend in a paintballing game, I'm certainly not thinking that she will be badly injured or killed. It's all part of a game that everyone has consented to play.

TIME TO REFLECT:

Do you and your colleagues agree on what is allowed in terms of weapon play?

CASE STUDY: MAKING IT TANGIBLE

Zoe Sills is Manager of the Earthtime Forest School nursery in Moray in the North of Scotland. The children are outdoors for around 90% of the time.

"All our staff love being outdoors," says Zoe, "they are passionate about it. It just wouldn't work otherwise."

The only area fenced off for safety is the yurt where children wait for their friends to arrive. An important part of Earthtime's ethos is encouraging connections with nature and each other. "It's about learning personal skills," says Zoe, "it's about wellbeing and the benefits of being outdoors. It's about skills like lighting fires and using tools."

On site are fire pits, wooden seesaws, tree stumps for climbing, rope swings, and loose parts such as pallets, tyres, plastic tubing, and drainpipes. The children have access to tinkering boxes containing pre-cut pieces of wood, nails, and small child-sized hammers. These are used with adult supervision and are very popular.

Part of Earthtime's ethos is around exposing the children to risk and allowing them to assess risk themselves.

The children are involved in the decision making, and we don't impose rules per se on what children are allowed to do. We discuss with them what they think the boundaries should be or what the limitations of a certain activity might be. Obviously, if it's fire, there are certain things they can and cannot do, and we are very tightly controlled on that. But again, we still put it back to the children: what do you think? Do you think we should do this or this? Why? Why is that important? That is part of the whole way we work: involving the children. There is never, ever a time when an adult in our setting will say to a child: "don't do that." It just doesn't happen. It might be: "Stop. Why did I stop you? What can you see happening here?" But there will always be discussion with the children about what we're doing and why. It is about them taking ownership. If you impose rules on a child, they may bother to listen to you, but they may not. If they come up with the rules themselves, they are far more likely to follow them. It's common sense.

The sessions are all child-led.

We very much hold back and only step in when asked or invited; when we see that by stepping in, we could extend their learning or an aspect of play or benefit that child by stepping in. That doesn't mean that we are standing around the outside, watch-

ing, with our arms folded. It's tricky, choosing that moment to step in. You spend a lot of time ready to step in but then not stepping in. It's very tempting to get involved. It's harder to hang back and wait and watch and see what happens.

Zoe is frequently asked about the nursery children climbing trees, particularly in terms of the permitted height. "A four-year-old doesn't understand how high two metres is, so we talk to the children, and we say, 'how high do you feel comfortable climbing?'"

Zoe stresses that it is all about the children making their own personal assessments. Children are given as much reassurance as they need. Adults don't make decisions for them but instead prompt the children to evaluate how comfortable they are.

We talk to them about their deeper emotions too: "Do you have that butterfly feeling in your tummy that means you are a little bit nervous? That probably means you want to come down. That might be as high as you are going to go." We make it tangible and relatable to them so they can identify the feelings for themselves.

Earthtime rarely receives any parental complaints because they are open from the start about their approach. Most parents appreciate the learning that takes place in the setting. "Just because the children are not sitting down with a pen and paper, does not mean we are not doing numeracy, literacy, science ... all of those things."

Zoe believes that an outdoor, child-led approach is needed for as long as possible:

> Balancing, climbing, and moving outdoors are the things that a child actually physically needs in order to sit still in a chair when they get to school. When you look at an early years class, and you see the children who are fidgety all the time and can't sit still, they haven't had that level of challenge – they need to move. It's not bad behaviour; they just can't do it.

Zoe has found significant benefits in terms of emotional wellbeing:

> Our children grow in confidence, and they are resilient: they pick themselves up and get on with it. A local outdoor organisation came and worked with the children with balance bikes, and the staff said: "Your children are the most amazing group to work with." The children at other nurseries didn't want to be outside for long; they got bored quickly and were upset if they fell off. Our children were totally up for anything. The organisers could just keep challenging our children and pushing them, and they would rise to it every time. It's when someone else brings their experience and recognises those differences that it really stands out for us. When you are immersed in it, you don't see it!

Conclusion

Children have the right to choose to play adventurously, and when we trust children and see them as competent and capable, they develop decision-making skills, sensory integration, motor function, resilience, confidence, and emotional regulation (Klein, 2016).

Crucially, adventurous play should be child-led. It's detrimental to children's wellbeing to unnecessarily restrict them or push them into taking risks they're not comfortable with.

TIME TO REFLECT:

- Are there any of Sandseter's categories that make you feel uncomfortable?
- Can you think of examples where children in your setting have challenged themselves during outdoor play?
- Where do children at your setting go outdoors to 'disappear'?
- Professor Brené Brown asks: "What's worth doing even if you fail?" Can you recall an emotional risk you took?

References

 Reading for children

Andreae, G., Parker-Rees, G. (2019). *Giraffes Can't Dance*. Solon: Findaway World, Llc.

Bright, R. and Field, J. (2018). *The Koala Who Could*. London: Orchard.

Browne, A. and Books, W. (1989). *The Tunnel*. London: Julia Macrae Books.

Reading for adults

Appleton, J. (1975). *The Experience of Landscape*. London: Wiley.

Armitage, M. (2012). Risky play is not a category – It's what children DO. [online] *Marc Armitage*. Available at: https://www.marc-arm itage.com/blog-archive/risky-play-is-not-a-category-its-what-chil dren-do_111s42 [Accessed 23 March 2021].

Caprino, F. (2018). When the risk is worth it: The inclusion of children with disabilities in free risky play. Available at: https://www.res earchgate.net/publication/338067931_When_the_risk_is_worth_i t_the_inclusion_of_children_with_disabilities_in_free_risky_play/ citation/download.

Carlson, F. (2009). Rough and tumble play 101. *Exchange: The Early Childhood Leaders' Magazine Since 1978*, 70–72.

Children's play and leisure: Promoting a balanced approach (Joint HSE/Play Safety Forum High Level Statement).

Cooley, C.H. (2017). *Human Nature and the Social Order*. S.L.: Routledge.

Dodd, H. and Lester, K. (2021). Adventurous play as a mechanism for reducing risk for childhood anxiety: A conceptual model. *Clin Child Fam Psychol Rev*, 24, 164–181. https://doi.org/10.1007/s10567-020 -00338-w

Frost, J. (2013). Why children climb. *Playground Professionals*. [online] playgroundprofessionals.com. Available at: https://playgroundpr ofessionals.com/playground/climbing-walls/why-children-climb [Accessed 9 February 2021].

Furedi, F. (1997). *Culture of Fear Risk-Taking and the Morality of Low Expectation*. London: Bloomsbury Publishing.

Gill, T. and Calouste Gulbenkian Foundation. (2007). *No Fear: Growing Up in a Risk Averse Society*. London: Calouste Gulbenkian Foundation.

Gladstone, A. (2016). *We're OK with Risky Play!* London: Lawrence Educational Publications.

Holland, P. (2008). *We Don't Play with Guns Here: War, Weapon and Superhero Play in the Early Years*. Philadelphia: Open University Press.

Jarvis, P. (2006). Rough and tumble play: Lessons in life. *Evolutionary Psychology*, 4, 330–346.

Keller, H. (1946). Let us have faith by Helen Keller [Chapter]. *Faith Fears Not*, Quote Page 50 and 51. Garden City: Doubleday & Company. (Verified with scans of 1946 reprint of 1940 edition).

Klein, J. and Ted Conferences (2016). *Our Relationship to Risk | Judy Klein | TEDxTahoeCity*. [online] www.youtube.com. Available at: https://www.youtube.com/watch?v=WAsW3TFdjlQ&ab_channel =TEDxTalks [Accessed 23 March 2021].

Moore, M.R. and Sabo-Risley, C. (2017). *Play in American Life: Essays in Honour of Joe L. Frost*. Bloomington: Archway Publishing.

Moorewood, G.D. (2014). Educating for life. *Inclusion Now Magazine*. Alliance for Inclusive Education, Summer 2014.

Morrongiello, B., Zdzieborski, D. and Normand, J. (2010). Understanding gender differences in children's risk taking and injury: A comparison of mothers' and fathers' reactions to sons and daughters misbehaving in ways that lead to injury. *Journal of Applied Developmental Psychology - J APPLIED DEV PSYCHOLOGY*, 31(4), 322–329. doi:10.1016/j.appdev.2010.05.004

Sandseter, E.B.H. (2010). It tickles in my tummy! *Journal of Early Childhood Research*, 8(1), 67–88.

Sandseter, E.B.H. (2010). Scaryfunny - A qualitative study of risky play among preschool children. Available at: https://www.researchgate. net/publication/236986868_Scaryfunny_-_A_qualitative_study_o f_risky_play_among_preschool_children.

Scott, E. and Panksepp, J. (2003). Rough-and-tumble play in human children. *Aggressive Behavior*, 29(6), 539–551.

Shakespeare, T. (2004). Social models of disability and other life strategies. *Scandinavian Journal of Disability Research*, 6(1), 8–21.

Solly, K. (2015). *Risk, Challenge and Adventure in the Early Years: A Practical Guide to Exploring and Extending Learning Outdoors*. London: Routledge.

Vasileva, V. (2018). The educator's role in supporting non-gendered play in early childhood education settings. *Children and Young People's Play, Children's Research Digest*, 5(2).

Relationships matter
The role of the adult

> Wellbeing themes in this chapter:
>
> Agency…Communication…Relationships…Inclusion…
> Partnership…Trust

Introduction

We can't overlook or underestimate the role of adults in children's lives (Gol-Guven, 2017). What we do matters and, when I look back, relationships form the background to every significant experience. To develop social and emotional competence, children need warm, responsive relationships (Roberts, 2010). I still clearly remember being trusted by my Reception teacher to look after our class guinea pig but then silently panicking as she placed this wriggly creature into my outstretched hands. Without a word, she looked at me with such confidence that I decided perhaps I could do this! Our day-to-day interactions affect how children view their own competence.

This relationship building takes time. Unfortunately, the way that the curriculum is interpreted in some settings means that taking the time to tune into children is not always valued.

> *"SLT make me feel guilty if I'm not constantly 'doing' something with the children."* Reception teacher

DOI: 10.4324/9781003137023-5

Tips for developing social and emotional competence in outdoor play:

- Show children unconditional positive regard. Listen without judgement.
- Enable and encourage children to try new ways to play (without forcing them to leave a task they are absorbed by).
- Accept and acknowledge children's feelings. Play can be exciting, frustrating, and even frightening. Talk about what you see and explore these feelings.
- Help children make and maintain friendships. Friendship building can be complicated, and there are lots of different skills involved. Our rope swing area is great for building social skills because children need to communicate, take turns, and listen carefully. (They tell each other exactly how hard they want to be pushed!) Just bear in mind that children want to play alone sometimes, and that is their right. Every child must be treated as an individual.

- Support children to find the 'just right challenge.' My friend, Bob, who is an occupational therapist, aims to design therapeutic activities that are the 'just right challenge' – not too easy and not too difficult. The term was first used by the pioneering occupational therapist Dr A. Jean Ayres all the way back in 1970 (Ayres, 2005).
- Be available and present without taking over. When deciding whether or when to step in, put the child at the centre of your thinking. Will they benefit from you stepping in? Do they want you to? Do they need you to?
- Build trust by respecting children's choices about how they want to play and supporting them to make their own decisions.

We are partners in children's outdoor play and good partnerships are characterised by trust and respect. I used to manage community projects and I found that the best partnerships thrive when both sides feel secure but also able to grow and develop. Do you feel protected but also encouraged to thrive in your current role? It's an interesting question to consider.

Collaboration is another essential element of partnership, and young children are usually delighted when we join in with their play. There are times when we should be enthusiastic, collaborative play partners, as long as we remember that our role is co-explorer, not dictator!

> "We need to remember, as an adult 'doing play,' to occupy a different peda-gogic stance. Play provides opportunities for children to identify the things they need to process and to develop their own ways of doing that. They are making sense of what is going on in the world, and each child may need to do this in a different way. As adults, we can't do this for a class of 27 different children. Self-determined play should be just that, children deciding what they are doing, not second guessing what is expected of them." Ben Tawil

Keeping children as safe as necessary

> "A good supervisor walks really quickly and makes sure no-one is getting bullied and that everyone is having fun and not hurting anyone." Emily

It's part of our role to monitor the outdoor area for dangerous hazards, and this is a particular issue for practitioners using public or shared spaces. In the past, I've had to remove a syringe, cigarette butts, and, on one memorable occasion, part of a dead grass snake from outdoor play areas. Working with young children is a complex, sometimes overwhelming role, and pressure to prevent harm can cause adults to be overly surveillant. Working alongside children to support them to assess risk, and trusting  them to take risks in their play that challenge them appropriately, leads to healthy decision making. We need to be careful not to intervene too quickly.

The Health and Safety Executive (HSE, 2012) emphasises that play providers should deal with risk responsibly, sensibly, and proportionately, whilst allowing children to take part in challenging play opportunities. These are things that I check on a daily basis:

- Weather forecast.
- Gates and fences. Check that gates are closed and that fences don't have holes, gaps, or sharp edges.
- Dangerous plants. I've come across giant hogweed at one setting. This can cause burns, and if you inform the local authority they will remove it.
- Loose parts with sharp edges. This most commonly happens with our plastic crates, especially during winter as they start to crack and split.
- Animal faeces or dead animals.
- Rubbish that has blown in or been left behind by unwanted visitors.
- Padlocks on stores for adult tools and fire equipment.

It's important to remember that serious accidents are very unlikely. On the rare occasions when things do go wrong, a balanced, transparent review must be carried out (Health and Safety Executive, 2012).

Rules and boundaries

As an NQT, I worried that enforcing the rules would damage my relationship with pupils, but I found that the opposite was true. Consistency shows children that we love and care for them and that they are part of our community. However, children need to understand why each rule is in place. Children are much more likely to follow the rules if they understand the need for them and are involved in deciding on them. (They will then clearly explain to others why the rule is needed too!) Sometimes, you may want to renegotiate boundaries with the children.

Some of the rules around outdoor play that we have jointly decided in my setting are: only climb trees if an adult is close enough to supervise, keep large sticks below waist height, and only eat a few raspberries or blackberries from each bush – don't strip it. We also have specific rules for fire that the children must follow.

You can't avoid conflict in outdoor play (or in life), but early years practitioners are experts at anticipating it and preventing it. We know our children, after all. However, if we are conflict averse or automatically step in every time as arbitrator, children don't get experience of solving conflicts, which can be a heathy process. Children are often insightful when asked how things can be improved, and discussion helps children take responsibility. This is effective even with very young children, who need more support to express themselves and work through the strong emotions they are experiencing. If I do need to step in, these are some strategies I use:

- Stay calm. Children need to realise that conflict is normal. It can be useful to frame it as 'problem solving.' Think to yourself about what you would like the children to take away from this.
- Actively listen. I personally like to get on the same level as children rather than looming over them!
- Acknowledge how the children are feeling and help them label their feelings. (This can also help children empathise with each other.)
- Recap what they see as the main issue(s).
- Ask for ideas for solutions and discuss them. Decide on a solution together.
- Support children to practise conflict resolution: I can't be the only teacher who is imitated in role play! This is a safe way for children to explore conflict resolution with their peers and practise responses.

Rules without relationships are less likely to be followed. If we are overloaded with other tasks, we are less likely to invest quality time in supporting children to resolve conflict.

Connection

"What do the grown-ups do?"

"They just stand and look around." Connie

Healthy, nurturing relationships with peers, adults, and

the environment help children "understand, express, and modulate their thoughts, feelings and behaviours" (Murray et al., 2015). Children need us to pay attention to their cues and respond sensitively. If children feel they matter to us, they see themselves in a more positive way and are more likely to care about others. Children with emotional regulation difficulties particularly need trusting and secure relationships.

It can be difficult to achieve a balance between being attentive and taking over. If we are overly directive, children can just switch off, and that's when practitioners can start to believe that children don't know how to play – these children are just not used to playing independently.

Early years consultant Rosemary Roberts talks of the importance of adult 'companions' for children in their play, offering security and support, and acting as 'midwives' (Roberts, 2010). I had two very different midwife experiences. When my first child was born, there was an emergency in the next room, and the midwife only came into our room sporadically. She was brusque and didn't listen, and even told me I wasn't coping. She tried to inject me with pethidine against my will when what I actually needed was support and encouragement. She was undoubtedly overwhelmed with other tasks and the hospital was short-staffed but it was frightening for me. The second time around, the midwife observed me and listened to me, reflecting back what I was saying. She reassured me that I was strong enough to achieve this and that I was doing the best I could. She supported me to make my own choices and decisions. I felt powerful but I also valued her support.

Children's relationships with their peers are also crucial. Studies show that peer collaboration in play contributes to children's social, emotional, intellectual, and linguistic development and produces a sense of competence as well as feelings of belonging and usefulness (Jarvis et al., 2014). Children improve social skills through activities where there's a shared goal, and a wild space can be great for this. The children in my setting love building dens and bridges over ditches.

Autistic children are more vulnerable to loneliness (Humphrey, 2015), and a lack of awareness and understanding of autism can mean that acceptance of difference is reduced (Humphrey, 2015). However, younger children seem to be the most accepting of disability (Nikolaraizi et al., 2005 as cited in Humphrey, 2015) and when there is a whole-school commitment to inclusion, children have more positive attitudes towards disability (Humphrey, 2015).

Children with an attachment disorder may need particular support to feel fully included in play. 'Jon,' for example, needed me to be with him at all times during the first few weeks, and gradually allowed me to go to a different space if I left my lanyard with him. A child with attachment issues can feel helpless, disempowered, and disregarded (Watkins, 2020). Above all, time is needed in order to build trust.

TIME TO REFLECT:

How do you support children to build friendships during outdoor play?

Play time

Time is a recurring theme in this book, and we need to resist barriers such as a strong focus on adult-directed learning preventing children following their own lines of enquiry.

Time has become a scarce resource, and most adults feel they don't have enough time to fit in all they need to achieve. This is an adult problem but should not become a child problem. Part of our role is to fight for the ethos that we feel children need. What are your beliefs in terms of supporting children's wellbeing? Is there anything that restricts this on a day-to-day basis?

Adults also deserve and need time for play. Being playful relieves stress and makes life more enjoyable. Ash Perrin is founder and CEO of the Flying Seagull Project, a UK-based arts charity dedicated to spreading laughter and smiles to those in need:

Adults in offices should agree to finish work at 3pm on one day and take it in turns to ask their own children for suggestions of things to do in that two hours to make them feel more playful. Ask the kids – they know! It is preposterous to think that we as adults can teach children how to play. We need to facilitate and create spaces for them to play.

Collaborating in children's play and being a part of their world can actually put us into a playful mood, distracting us from worries and concerns. There's a reason we share with each other the funny or joyful moments we've observed – it makes work more pleasurable and rejuvenates us. (And those joyful moments come from us giving children time.)

TIME TO REFLECT:

The saying goes: "life is a journey, not a destination." How do you remain present?

Trust for the process

"Do you like it when the person supervising you plays and helps you, or if they just watch you?"
"What's supervised?"
(Explanation)
"Oh. I don't like to be supervised. Ever." Jack

When children have sufficient time to work things out and explore different ideas in their outdoor play, they develop decision-making skills. Studies show that children are more likely to be motivated and confident when we

value the process rather than the outcome (Meyer et al., 2008).

I remember watching a child on his first day at our nursery. He was holding a wooden plank with one hand, while trying to roll cars down it, but this was impossible to do at the same time. He put the plank on the floor and pushed the cars along it but was irritated by the lack of speed. I crouched down and looked at the plank with him. "I wonder how we could keep this end higher?" I pondered. "It goes down again!" He replied. I placed a small twig underneath and as I did this, he said: "no!" because he already knew it would snap. He thought about the problem then toddled unsteadily off to get a plastic crate. He lifted one end of the plank and placed it onto the crate. Wondering about it together helped his thinking process. If we see ourselves as the only source of learning, there is much less chance of metacognition – children learning how to learn.

Professor Mine Gol-Guven suggests: "what could be the most engaging, enjoyable, and flowable if not play?" She explains that autonomy is a vital feature of flow: children need independence to become lost in the moment. However, young children swiftly learn that no matter how deeply they are involved in an independent activity, there will be interruption by adults, for example to remind them of the rules (Gol-Guven, 2017).

I once visited a setting where the Reception children were required to stop their play and become completely silent every time the Headteacher walked in. The Headteacher praised the children for not moving a muscle and looking at her intently, even when she had simply come to pass on a private message to the class teacher. Take a moment to consider the message this conveys to children.

Pressures such as academic progress or a beautifully tidy outdoor area are adult problems, but they inevitably affect child–adult relationships. I once saw this exchange at a setting. A child was stacking a variety of different loose parts in one area of the playground. The teacher said, "what IS that?" Without waiting for a reply, the teacher commented: "you'll have to tidy that up soon." I saw the child visibly deflate. As the first adult left, a student teacher approached and said: "how's it going?" She crouched down at the child's level and looked genuinely interested. Then she simply waited.

It was a powerful interaction to watch. The child thought silently for a few moments. Then he explained that he was trying to get one part in place to finish his 'tower' but didn't know how to do it. The adult repeated back to him what she understood he had said, and the child suddenly saw a solution. This child experienced an adult's interest, not just in the outcome of his labours, but in the process. Our spoken language and body language tell a clear story to children.

TIME TO REFLECT:

Are there times when it might be beneficial to interrupt a child's outdoor play?

The things we say (and the things we show)

I remember feeling confused in one Reception playground by the way the children would run towards one area of the playground then abruptly stop and run off in the opposite direction. I couldn't work it out. After watching another child run close to that area then freeze and back away, I decided to ask him why. He pointed at the lunchtime supervisor and whispered: "She shouts at us if we go near there." The lunchtime supervisor patiently explained that the children couldn't possibly manage the three low steps leading to

another (empty) part of the playground. The children consequently associated that area with being shouted at.

The language we use sends a clear message to children about our view of their competence and it can give children power or cause a disconnect. For example, asking a child in the playground: "do your shoes feel OK?" is more helpful than saying: "your shoes are on the wrong feet. Come here. I'll swap them over." Motivating language and sensitive questioning can make all the difference. A three-year-old in our playground was bewildered by getting his foot caught in some netting. I asked him to tell me what the problem was. He replied: "I pushed it *(foot)* through the hole but now it's too big ... 'cause ... the shoe." I said: "So you pushed your shoe through the hole and now you can't get the shoe back through the hole?" He nodded and wiggled his trapped foot and then exclaimed: "I can take my shoe off! Then pull my foot." Off came the shoe, out came the foot, and the shoe went back on again. Here is our competence training ground once again. He was able to be reflective and talk through the steps to success. Fundamental to self-awareness is learning from mistakes. He learned that his shoe goes through netting but is more difficult to pull out again!

Facilitating deeper thinking in outdoor play requires sensitivity. Headteacher Julie Jones explains:

It's about bringing that buzz through open questioning which extends the play. We need to allow the child to run with their line of enquiry and fully explore it, but also be ready to say: "I wonder what would happen if...?" Be there as a co-explorer and remain curious. This is a process that is built over time until it becomes established. When you are in a setting where adults don't normally co-explore, then children's play can completely change when an adult joins them. I've seen a child stop playing when an adult comes and sits next to them because the child accepts that someone with more knowledge and competency is going to tell them how it should be done. We want children to be comfortable to fail and carry on, and we need to sow those seeds very early on. The adult should be a co-learner, enquiring with them.

This is sustained shared thinking (SST): "an episode in which two or more individuals work together in an intellectual way to solve a problem, clarify a concept, evaluate activities, extend a narrative etc. Both parties must contribute to the thinking" (Iram Siraj-Blatchford et al., 2002).

Even if you haven't heard the term, you've certainly facilitated sustained shared thinking – those problem-solving conversations where there's a healthy to-and-fro without anyone dominating. We're back to time again. Time to tune into children and value their thoughts. These conversations help us challenge children by guiding them into thinking more deeply, but studies have shown that practitioners cannot effectively facilitate this if they are overloaded with tasks (Purdon, 2014).

As well as the verbal language we use, our body language also tells a story. Excitement and curiosity are infectious and, conversely, even very young children pick up on boredom, indifference, or frustration.

> ## TIME TO REFLECT:
>
> Can you think of an adult you worked with whose body language was closed and discouraging? How did it make you feel working with that person?

Support to process and practise

Shortly after schools reopened more widely after lockdown in June 2020, I was with a group of Reception children in a wild natural area. Some began

being 'chasers,' running after others and making low sounds with their arms outstretched. Some shouted "it's the virus!" Those being chased screamed and ran away but returned if the chasers were too slow. The children were all visibly delighted by this game, which captured the interest of the whole group for 12 minutes then abruptly stopped. The children then became very quiet. Some lay down on the grass, touching each other's hands. It was fascinating to watch, and seemed to be a way to make sense of a confusing and unsettling aspect of their lives.

Play is a natural way for children to feel big emotions, express them, and process them. One morning during my NQT year, I caught sight of a familiar face in the playground. Karen and I had worked together in the past, and we discussed how exciting it was that I would be teaching her son, Bobby. However, by the time Bobby started in my class, Karen had died. Children can often present challenging, anxious, or withdrawn behaviour as a result of trauma, and research has shown that play activates feel-good hormones, opioids, and oxytocin, releasing feelings of calm. Bobby was at his most relaxed and calm playing outdoors.

Observing children's play can tell us a lot about how they're feeling, and play enables all children to practice being in an uncomfortable situation. One of my pupils often plays "dogs" despite being terrified of them – for her, it's an effective way to process these fears.

Having the time to experience and process his emotions through different types of play helped Bobby begin to come to terms with this life-changing experience. Much of the time, outdoor play simply enabled Bobby to unreservedly be himself: running, shouting, jumping, laughing. Even when children are facing the unthinkable, they still need the opportunity to be a child. In fact, at this time, they need it more than ever.

TIME TO REFLECT:

How do you see the role of nature in children working through emotions?

Observing outdoor play

"When children are playing, they cannot help but show you what is going on in their minds. If you are not thinking about the next ten targets or what you are doing in the next half hour, if you are watching or observing, being alongside the child, they will show you. It is about enabling the child to express themselves." Dr Sharie Coombes

By tuning into children's play, we can build secure and caring relationships, and this is the time when young children often make their feelings clear. Using the Leuven Scales can help us identify wellbeing indicators such as concentration and enthusiasm so that we can adapt the outdoor provision if necessary. Noticing repeated patterns of behaviour helps us make provision for schemas such as transporting or connecting. For example, when I recently observed June playing outside, she spent the whole morning carrying conkers and wooden 'coins' from a cable reel into a tipi. She was entirely focused on her task and hummed happily to herself. When another child entered the tipi,

June told her: "I got the treasure!" They then began to carefully sort the items. I put a wheelbarrow and some small baskets nearby, and June proceeded to fill the baskets with pine cones and then put them in the wheelbarrow, which she then wheeled to the tipi. Seeing a child's interactions with their peers gives us a more rounded picture of that child. Later that day, June persuaded a small group of younger children from the nursery to help her transport the loose parts and it was interesting to see her in the role of leader.

Observing children at play requires a sensitive approach. Ms. Cheng Xueqin, founder of the Anji Play Philosophy and Approach, instructs that adults should approach children's play with: "mouth shut, hands down, eyes, ears and heart open to discover the child" (Xueqin, n.d.).

In my first term as a student teacher, I watched the play outside completely change when a besuited Ofsted inspector advanced, clipboard in hand. The children were aware that something out of the ordinary was going on and hesitated in their play, afraid to do the wrong thing. (The inspector made it very obvious that he was not comfortable around four-year-olds outside with paintbrushes and soon disappeared!) If children don't feel comfortable, we're less likely to get insightful information.

Supporting children to record their own experiences gives us their perspective, and in my class we have regular 'look at me!' sessions where the child views film or photo footage of their play and responds to it. They are always excited to provide accompanying 'narration.' However, it's important not to let the technology get in the way of human interactions.

Ben Tawil talks of the artistry of the play worker unobtrusively observing play:

> I was watching a group of children trying to create a habitat for a frog they had found. They had dug a hole by a tree, and they kept pouring water into the hole, and the water would simply disappear. I watched them, and one child had run back to the outdoor tap and filled a big bucket. This boy was struggling, carrying these big buckets. I thought to myself "how long do I feign incompetence before it starts to become harmful to the children?" I was pushing a wheelbarrow around and collecting rubbish off the floor, doing a litter pick while listening and watching all the time. A small sheet of plastic conveniently fell out of my wheelbarrow by the tree, and a child immediately shouted: "what if we put this in the bottom of it?" That is the artistry. It is covert observation and supervision, and facilitation of the play, while resisting adulteration.

TIME TO REFLECT:

Can you think of other ways to give children more ownership of the observation process? How do you involve parents and carers?

Enabling participation

"Children are undoubt-edly the most photo-graphed, and the least listened to members of society." (Hart, 1997)

This quote is from an essay on children's participation by sociologist Roger Hart, written in 1992 when mobile phones with a camera were rare. Unfortunately, it seems even more relevant today. Reports state that children living in the 41 wealthiest countries feel unable to fully participate in decision making at home or school (UNICEF, 2020).

In his essay, Hart included a diagram of the 'ladder of participation,' a tool to assess children's levels of participation in projects. He believed that adults should plan to maximise the

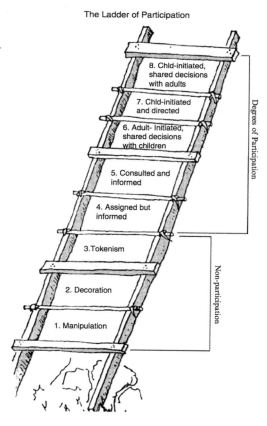

The Ladder of Participation

8. Chld-initiated, shared decisions with adults

7. Chld-initiated and directed

6. Adult- Initiated, shared decisions with children

5. Consulted and informed

4. Assigned but informed

3.Tokenism

2. Decoration

1. Manipulation

Degrees of Participation

Non-participation

opportunities for any child to be able to participate, if they wish to, at the highest level of his or her ability (Hart, 1997).

I've adapted Hart's levels slightly to make it less project-focused and added examples of outdoor play, and you can see this in Table 5.1.

Table 5.1 Hart's ladder of participation

Manipulation: this is the lowest rung of the ladder. Children do or say what the adults suggest they do, or children are consulted but given no feedback.	Hart gives the example of adults asking children to draw their ideal playground without intending to use their ideas.
Decoration: children take part but they don't fully understand the context and have no say.	A teacher encourages each child to come and make some chalk marks outside which eventually makes a large pattern to celebrate Diwali.
Tokenism: children are asked what they think but have little or no choice about communicating their views.	Children are asked about their favourite outdoor play activity for a display. This is not reflected in the activities that are provided outside.
Assigned but informed: adults decide on a play activity and children want to take part. The children understand the intentions and adults respect their views.	A teacher tells the children that there will be a water play day. The children are enthusiastic and want to take part.
Consulted and informed: adults design and run the play activities, but children's views are taken seriously.	Adults set out different activities outside but are also responsive to children's suggestions for different equipment to be provided.
Adult initiated: shared decisions with children. This is true participation. Although adults put out the play equipment, the decision making is shared with children.	Adults ask the children as a group what they would like to have available outside and allow children the time to think and be heard.
Child initiated and directed: children have the initial ideas and adults are available but do not take charge.	The equipment outside is all easily accessible for children to get out and use in their play. Adults scaffold play if necessary and respond to invitations to become involved.
Child initiated: shared decisions with adults. Children have the ideas, set up the play, and invite adults to join them in making decisions.	A child has enjoyed painting on an easel outside but now wants to paint on a bigger scale. She suggests that they stretch a large roll of paper across the playground for collaborative painting and asks the adult for ideas for securing it so that it doesn't blow away.

As practitioners, we might regularly use a range of the approaches you see in this table, but for emotional health, every child needs to know that they have the choice to participate at the highest level, regardless of their circumstances or abilities. We need high expectations for children and a belief in their capacity to participate, and we need to value difference, remove barriers to participation, and challenge discriminatory practice (Nutbrown et al., 2013).

Let's enable all children to be decision makers and change makers. How do we find out the views of very young children or those with limited verbal skills? It's about developing strong trusting relationships with each child and their family.

Every child has something to say – we just need to hear that voice, rather than basing outdoor provision on our assumptions. Cowgate Under 5's Centre is fully committed to enabling children to choose how they participate, and you can read about their approach in the following case study.

TIME TO REFLECT:

How can we enable more child-initiated processes and activities?

CASE STUDY: FREEDOM WITH GUIDANCE

Dr Lynn McNair is the manager of the Cowgate Under 5's Centre, a nursery that follows a process-orientated, play-based curriculum.

Having the child at the centre of their thinking is fundamental to the approach at Cowgate. Dr McNair comments:

> We are Froebellian in our approach and Froebel talks about "freedom with guidance." This is a good thing to have in your head when working with children, supporting children's freedom, and respecting their agency. Our focus is always the child. The pedagogical encounters with children are really rich and we put that before anything else.

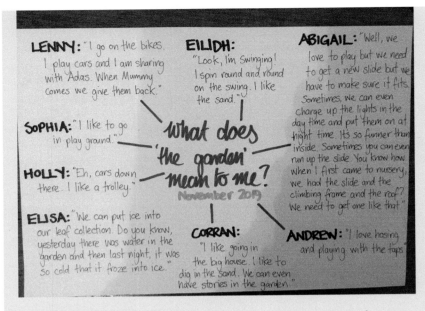

Dr McNair feels strongly that part of our role is to speak up if systems are not for the benefit of the child:

> When you know things are wrong, you have to fight back. If you don't do that, you're kind of living a lie. I would encourage people to stand back and question what they are doing and why they are doing it. What we need is people who will actually challenge and question the status quo, and we have a staff team that does that. They want to make a difference in children's lives and they know that I will also fight back. The truth is, decisions are not always made in the children's best interests.

Dr McNair emphasises the importance of asking ourselves, as practitioners, how we see the child:

> We need to see the richness and resourcefulness of children. What is key for me, is having in our heads this trust for children and belief in their capabilities. If a child is climbing a tree for example, and you have this knowledge of who this child is as an individual, then you know whether to step in and offer verbal

support or physical support or to step back. This only comes from knowing who children really are. It isn't about treating children as part of a homogeneous group. In order to really support children, you first of all have to understand them. That can seem a really basic way of thinking but actually it is quite complex.

Dr McNair points out that connecting with parents helps complete the picture: "You have to take a holistic view, you have to understand what's happening at home, you need to understand who the child is in the setting and connect both of them."

Sometimes, as Dr McNair points out, others may not be comfortable respecting the child's choices:

> Most of our children take their shoes and socks off, but we had one child who did this all the time in winter. We said to visitors: 'this is who she is.' That was her identity, that was her personality. Why would we make her wear shoes?

At times, this can lead to challenging conversations with parents:

> Say for example a child wants to go outdoors without their coat on and the parent wants them to wear a coat, we would go with what the child is saying. Their coats aren't far away so they can get their coat if they need it. It's about trusting the child. We've put our foot down quite a few times. We are pretty strong in our beliefs and how we are with children.

Choice is key to Cowgate's ethos. For example, the children choose whether or not they go to the nature kindergarten or an outdoor space every day, rather than adults selecting children. Dr McNair is very clear on the negative connotations of the word 'allow,' preferring to use the word 'enable.'

> Who has the power there? As a staff, we talk about adults being aware that they have the power, and negotiating power all the time. It's about living alongside the children. Our staff is a flattened hierarchy, so the staff make decisions alongside children. Our principles underpin everything we do. If it wouldn't marry with our principles, it won't be happening.

Children are also at the centre of resourcing the outdoor area:

> Children lead the way and our staff team are really tuned into the perspective of the child. Listening to what they are saying all the time and responding to that is key to how we set up any aspect of the nursery. Our outdoor environment rarely changes, only if children indicate there needs to be a change. Everything is quite natural. It's very rare for us to have plastic, very rarely do we have bought resources. Children bring things in from the woods. We don't set anything up. We trust the children, their agency, their leadership. When we say that children are leading the way, we really mean it.

A key part of the centre's success is the reflective approach of the staff:

> We've got to keep looking at ourselves, reflecting and applying reflexivity. We've got to be aware of that internal scrutiny of ourselves. It's fundamentally this relationship between the child and the adult and this knowing that enables the relationship to be a really rich and deep one.

Playing in partnership

"I like it when the adults play with me, not just watch me." Zayden

Most young children want adults to take notice of their play, and they often invite adults in. Ben Tawil feels we should see this as a privilege and a responsibility:

You are an adopted child who has been invited into their play. That is an incredibly special opportunity, and you need to remember your role. If you play with children meaningfully, you value their play. Equally, if you play with them and you are distracted by all the things you have to do, you send the opposite message. They know you are feigning interest and you don't think their play is valuable.

I can remember desperately wanting to join in with games on the playground but not always having the confidence. Sometimes, children need us to help them join in with their peers, without us controlling the play. Following the child's lead and being curious and responsive enables children to grow, and this process takes time.

Early years specialist and author Greg Bottrill calls for a rejection of the government tick list in favour of whole-hearted participation in children's play:

> Children are magical. They see things completely differently to us. If children invite us into their play, we are walking through the door into their adventures. Do you choose to go through the door, or do you just stand at the side of the door and watch what happens? If you are standing there with a clipboard, children will see through you. When you are authentically within the play, you are researching the play, and you will get the observations you need. It's magical transference. We need to move beyond the grey area of objectives and teachers controlling children and move into the joy of living.

Conclusion

The adult's role in outdoor play is important and complex. It's much more than simply supervising. Play has been described as what young children do when adults do not direct them, and children need us to support their independence and help them become more capable and competent.

But we are social creatures. We don't live in a vacuum. We need human connections to feel good about ourselves. The early relationships that young children have with practitioners are fundamental, and feeling loved and listened to is central to wellbeing (Office for National Statistics, 2020). Outdoor play is an essential journey for young children, and they need us with them on that journey.

TIME TO REFLECT:

- Who do you share observations with?
- What are your beliefs and values around outdoor play? Do your own memories of play influence them?
- Why do you think professionals sometimes underestimate the capabilities of young children?
- How can we ensure that children playing in the outdoor area achieve increased emotional competence?
- How much of your time is regularly taken up with tasks that do not benefit the children?

References

 Reading for children

Llenas, A. (2018). *The Colour Monster*. London: Templar Publishing.

 Reading for adults

Attwood, T. (2007). *The Complete Guide to Asperger's Syndrome*. London: Jessica Kingsley Publishers.

Ayres, J. (2005). *Sensory Integration and the Child: Understanding Hidden Sensory Challenges*. 25th Anniversary Edition. Los Angeles: Western Psychological Services.

Brodie, K. (2014). *Sustained Shared Thinking in the Early Years: Linking Theory to Practice*. London: Routledge.

Fisher, J. (2016). *Interacting or Interfering?: Improving the Quality of Interactions in the Early Years*. Maidenhead: Open University Press.

Garvey, D. (2018). *Nurturing Personal, Social and Emotional Development in Early Childhood: A Practical Guide to Understanding Brain Development and Young Children's Behaviour.* London: Jessica Kingsley Publishers.

Gol-Guven, M. (2017). Play and flow: Children's culture and adults' role. *Erken Çocukluk Çalışmaları Dergisi,* 1(2), 194. doi:10.24130/eccd-jecs.196720171230

Hart, R.A. (1997). *Children's Participation: The Theory and Practice of Involving Young Citizens in Community Development and Environmental Care.* London: Earthscan Publications.

Health and Safety Executive. (2012). *Children's Play and Leisure – Promoting a Balanced Approach.* Available at: https://www.hse.gov.uk/entertainment/childrens-play-july-2012.pdf.

Humphrey, N. (2015). *School, Teacher and Support Staff Issues in Autism Education.* Los Angeles: Sage Reference.

Iram Siraj-Blatchford and Department for Education and Skills. (2002). *Researching Effective Pedagogy in the Early Years.* Nottingham: Dept. For Education and Skills.

Jarvis, P., Newman, S. and Swiniarski, L. (2014). On 'becoming social': The importance of collaborative free play in childhood. *International Journal of Play,* 3(1), 53–68. doi:10.1080/21594937.2013.863440

Meyer, B., Haywood, N. and Sachdev, D. (2008). *Independent Learning, Literature Review.* Nottingham: The Department for Children, Schools and Families.

Murray, D. W., Rosanbalm, K., Christopoulos, C., and Hamoudi., A. 2015. Self-regulation and toxic stress: Foundations for understanding self-regulation from an applied developmental perspective. *OPRE Report* # 2015-21.

Nutbrown, C., Clough, P. and Atherton, F. (2013). *Inclusion in the Early Years.* London: Sage.

Office for National Statistics. (2020). *Children's Views on Well-Being and What Makes a Happy Life, UK: 2020 A Qualitative Analysis of Children's Perspectives on Their Well-Being and What Makes a Happy Life for a Child Using UK Wide Focus Groups.* Available at:

https://www.ons.gov.uk/peoplepopulationandcommunity/wellbein
g/articles/childrensviewsonwellbeingandwhatmakesahappylifeuk
2020/2020-10-02.

Purdon, A. (2014). Sustained shared thinking in an early childhood
setting: An exploration of practitioners' perspectives. *Education
3-13*, 44, 1–14. doi:10.1080/03004279.2014.907819

Roberts, R. (2010). *Wellbeing from Birth*. London: Sage.

UNICEF Innocenti. (2020). *Worlds of Influence: Understanding What
Shapes Child Well-Being in Rich Countries,* Innocenti Report Card
16. UNICEF Office of Research – Innocenti, Florence.

Watkins, S. (2020). How to support children with attachment disorders
| A Unique Child. [online] *Teach Early Years*. Available at: https:
//www.teachearlyyears.com/a-unique-child/view/how-to-support
-children-with-attachment-disorders [Accessed 10 February 2021].

Winnicott, D.W. (2017). *Playing and Reality*. London: Taylor & Francis
Ltd.

Xueqin, C. (n.d.). A parent and advocates guide to Anji play. [online]
Anji Play. Available at: http://www.anjiplay.com/guide [Accessed 10
February 2021].

Honesty and love

Wellbeing themes in this chapter:

Attachment…Belonging…Communication…Empathy… Inclusion…Trust

"What I love about the school is the communication. The communication to the parents is as good as the communication to the children. The communication is about honesty and love." Pamela Chisholm, parent

Introduction

"Generally, for a child to flourish and achieve in school, they need to feel that they belong and are a valued part of the school community. School belonging or school connectedness involves feeling personally accepted, respected, included, and supported by others." (Goodenow, 1993)

I changed primary schools when I was ten, and my new teacher made it clear that my family were outsiders. We were the only vegetarians in the village and didn't own a TV (the TV licence man couldn't get his head round this!). My dad had long hair and we'd go on CND marches. On one memorable family outing, we joined a tour of Sellafield nuclear power plant and were swiftly removed when my dad started to ask difficult questions. We wild camped in the Black Mountains, swimming in icy clear streams and cooking over a campfire. My childhood was the best

DOI: 10.4324/9781003137023-6

possible start in terms of healthy physical and emotional development, but my teacher made it clear from day one that my family were 'other.' Her snide comments in class about our lifestyle made it impossible for me to trust her.

Children need to feel they belong, and we are privileged to be able to create a culture where children feel loved and included, and where families feel involved and welcomed. It's not all plain sailing of course, and the relationship between parents and settings can sometimes be fraught: strong relationships require time and effort. But when it works, it works for everybody.

In this chapter, when I use the term 'parent,' I am referring to a child's main caregivers.

Parents: the decisive influence

"Daddy doesn't mind if I get covered in mud. He is proud when I try climbing new things." Edie

"If you are lucky enough to be a parent, you need to play with your children." Ash Perrin, Flying Seagull

The level of nurture and responsiveness that a child receives from their primary caregivers affects how they cope later in life (Shonkoff and Phillips, 2000). Experience of secure attachment enables children to trust others, and builds confidence, self-regulation, and empathy, as well as the ability to support others (Garvey, 2018, p. 105).

So secure attachment is important not only for a child's healthy emotional development, but also for the healthy functioning of a nurturing community (Siegel, 2001). This means we have a double role: creating secure attachment with the children we work with and supporting families in their attachment with their children (Gillespie and Hunter, 2011). Outdoor play provides ideal opportunities for this, and studies show that complex play interactions between parents and infants lead to better social skills and more healthy play interactions with other children (Vandell and Wilson, 1987).

Inviting parents to outdoor play sessions helps us learn more about the child and also model healthy interactions. This modelling could include:

- Facilitating conflict resolution.
- Being engaged and collaborating.

- Picking up on cues during play.
- Joining in with play without dominating.
- Extending a child's thinking.
- Supporting schematic play.

Children's early experiences influence their views on outdoor play, and if a parent obviously feels uncomfortable outside in nature, a child will pick up on this. However, when children are excited about emotionally healthy outdoor play, they don't keep it to themselves!

> "The children come home happy and excited to tell you what they've done. They are excited to carry on with the things they're learning outdoors. My wee boy, Ben, constantly repeats the phrase: 'muddy hands, happy hearts,' a motto that they use in school." Pamela Chisholm

TIME TO REFLECT:

How can you support parents to be more playful?

Ceangal: parents as partners

Children are much more likely to thrive and feel confident when there's a strong partnership between parents and a setting (Wheeler and Connor et al., 2009), and parents are the experts on their own child. It's worth remembering that we want the best for children and most parents do too – when parents seem aggressive or unreasonable, they're often just acting as powerful advocates for their child (although this can be uncomfortable to deal with).

On New Year's Eve, minutes before the start of 2020, I was in Dublin, surrounded by jubilant revellers. I spotted a poster on the wall with the word 'Ceangal' (*pronounced 'key-angle'*). "What does that mean?" I shouted to a group of people nearby. "Connection!" one of them shouted back, giving me a hug, "you know, linking together!"

Outdoor play can help us to build 'ceangal' with parents. Studies show that practitioners influence parental beliefs (Wheeler and Connor et al., 2009), and sharing research on the wellbeing benefits of outdoor play can be powerful. As a teacher, I've always shared the reasons behind our approaches to maths or phonics, but I've only recently started sharing research on outdoor play and wellbeing. Most parents don't have time to wade through academic papers, but a few key findings can be presented alongside an eye-catching image in a blog or newsletter or via social media. Pitch it right so that it is easily understood but not patronising. This approach is mutually beneficial because it prompts us to re-examine how and why we do what we do.

A true collaborative partnership isn't about one-way communication. Elinor Goldschmied, who first used the term 'key person,' talks of the "triangle of trust and communication" between the child, the parent, and the practitioner (Goldschmied and Sellack, 1996). When everyone in that triangle feels trusted, they are better able to authentically be themselves and learn from each other.

Sometimes parents can be play change agents at a setting, and their support is often invaluable. I've had parents build wooden structures, create mud kitchens, plant trees, donate loose parts, fundraise for wet weather gear, and run inspiring outdoor play sessions. Partnership is not just about maintaining the equilibrium, and sometimes parents have prompted me to look at issues around outdoor play in a completely different way.

There are multiple benefits of good parent partnership around play:

- A shared understanding of how the child develops.
- Better inclusion. To avoid discriminatory practice, we need to know as much about each child as possible so that any barriers to fully participatory play can be removed.
- Children feel more settled and are challenged appropriately in their play.
- Different perspectives are shared.
- Wider community understanding of the benefits of outdoor play.

Working to help families feel trusted and empowered can also create powerful play advocates in the local community. I once visited a setting that was receiving numerous noise complaints from two residents living right next to the school. The situation was resolved when another local resident, who had been volunteering at the school, wrote a polite and positive letter in response, detailing how much her autistic child gains from outdoor play.

TIME TO REFLECT:

How do you share research on outdoor play with parents?

Reconnecting

"Parents want children to get more fresh air but complain if they get dirty." Emily

Barriers that prevent parents from actively engaging with a setting include:

- Lack of time.
- Pressure from work.
- Living on a low income.
- Single parent status.
- Illness, depression, or disability within the family (Wheeler and Connor et al., 2009).

Parents may also have negative associations with education settings, and the fact that early years settings are predominantly staffed by women can make fathers feel particularly conspicuous (Wheeler and Connor et al., 2009). Most adults have good memories of outdoor play, so joining an outdoor play workshop can be less intimidating than joining a classroom-based activity. You can also show parents that sessions don't have to involve making 25 identical versions of the same craft. (Just warn parents to come in old clothes!) Encouraging parents to share their memories of play with the children can be powerful. This could be done virtually but it has a bigger impact if adults can model outdoors how they used to play. A good way to bring everyone together at the end of a session is to use parachute play – it stimulates so many aspects of emotional learning, from teamwork to emotional regulation. Those holding the parachute have to co-operate and communicate with each other. Parachute play can be wildly exciting but also calming, and using it in different ways enables children to experience and process lots of different emotions.

Clear communication is fundamental to strong relationships and being open from the start about your approach to outdoor play helps prevent complaints. It makes life easier if you can refer parents to a play policy where your ethos is set out: when parents have all the information they need and are clear that 'this is how we do things here,' there is less room for misunderstanding. This also ensures that staff are on-board. The policy needs to be simple and straightforward and accessible to all.

Unfortunately, even with the best communication, there will still be complaints from time to time. Make sure you have support to protect your own wellbeing, particularly if the complainant is known to be aggressive. Parents can sometimes voice their fears in a challenging way that feels undermining, and it can be difficult to remain calm in this situation. Simply dismissing a parent's fears is counterproductive, just as it is harmful to reply to an anxious child climbing a tree: "no, you're not scared!" After all, it's a parent's job to protect their children from harm. Sometimes, you might become aware of critical comments second-hand, and I prefer to tackle these head-on, inviting parents in to discuss the problem, so that the issue doesn't escalate. Parents sometimes just need to be heard, and their anger or upset may be rooted in an emotional wellbeing issue.

From my experience, the main aspects of outdoor play that generate complaints are: the lack of an end product, messy play, and safety. The paper 'Muddy Knees and Muddy Needs' highlights the fact that while most parents are aware of the benefits of outdoor play, many still find it difficult to accept that 'real learning' doesn't always take place in a classroom through a teacher-led activity. Being outdoors is often seen as an opportunity for children to simply 'let off steam' (Parsons and Traunter, 2020). Generally, though, parents are persuaded by seeing the positive ways in which their children are progressing through play.

Messy play can be a thorny issue. Life is hectic and busy parents can feel stressed about having to wash muddy clothes. Some parents associate dirt and mess with neglect and feel pressure to keep their children clean at all times. This message can be passed onto children, who are then afraid to get dirty. Having wet weather gear for every child helps, as well as reinforcing the message that this is healthy, safe practice that the children enjoy, so spare clothes are essential.

"With the clothing at school, there is a real ethos of one for all and all for one. The school never makes a child feel left out. I love that about the school." Pamela Chisholm

If parents feel their child is unsafe during outdoor play, this can lead to difficult conversations. However, if you believe in your approach and explain it, backing it up with your policies, parents will usually take the time to listen, especially if their child is passionate about outdoor play.

"My son has grown outside. Learning through play is great because if the children are happy, it's easier to get them to understand things. They don't even realise they are learning. His confidence is so high, there's no fear. The confidence it's given him is immense." Pamela Chisholm

It's not a failing to compromise sometimes and it's good to give time and space to parents' opinions, but you also need to be clear on your values. You might want to make some things non-negotiable, such as when children have access to the outdoors or having a change of clothes in every day. Parents appreciate clear communication, so set out your stall from the start.

Sometimes, the disconnect between parent and educator is psychological. Social media can make practitioners increasingly feel judged and consequently anxious that parents won't approve of certain play behaviours. If you have the support of those in authority at your setting, it's much easier to feel secure about your ethos and communicate this to parents.

TIME TO REFLECT:

How do the views of parents affect outdoor play at your setting?

CASE STUDY: OUTDOORS IS WHERE THEY FIND THEIR VOICE

Ashleigh Robertson is acting Principal Teacher at Ravenswood School. She and her phase partner, Laura Simpson, are committed to child-led outdoor play and have success-fully persuaded parents of the benefits. The school uses a local wooded area called the Ravenswood Marsh on their 'Ranger Days,' and they go out in all weathers. Initially, the Ranger Days were just for the youngest children, but the scheme has gradually been  rolled out across the whole school.

"Our big play journey started a couple of years ago," says Ashleigh, "my phase leader and I were doing a lot of research and we felt that we were at a point where we were offering really good play indoors, and we wanted to take this outdoors too."

The teachers follow the interests of the children: "for example, last week the children were really interested in the water, and that led onto building bridges and trying to cross the water. The week before that it was dens. We let the children lead it." From time to time, Ashleigh introduces a storyline going on in the background, and she occasionally plans a stand-alone activity, but there is no expectation that every child has to take part.

> Sometimes, it's just a little provocation that sets them off on a journey. The children always take it where you would never have imagined. I just love that. If everything outside was structured, that would just kill the imagination, wouldn't it? I'd rather children were engaged in quality play and made a mess than finding an area pristine at the end of the day.

Initially, Ashleigh and Laura were unsure about how much freedom to allow the children.

> How would we ensure they stay safe and how would we make sure that none of the children gets lost in this wooded area? There were risks. However, we've seen children really improve in terms of their own risk assessment. When I compare them from the start of term to now, they are so much better at thinking: "that bit is covered in mud, it's really slippy" or "I'm too high, and I might fall, so I'm going to try a different way of doing that." They say to each other: "watch out, that log's broken, you can't stand on it, you could fall." They do their own risk assessing, and they determine if it's safe. If it's not safe, they work out a way to make it safer.

The less outgoing pupils have really benefitted.

> We found that the quieter children found their voice outside. In class, those children didn't like taking the lead and preferred to be observers and stand back. They were not keen to problem

solve on their own, and they would often come and ask for help. Those same children, when they went outside, it was like they were completely different children. You could have the quietest children indoors, but the minute you take them outdoors, they'd be saying to their peers "no, I think you should do it like this! Let's try this!" or "that isn't going to work for the den because it isn't long enough. Let's try this. Oh, I've got an idea." Outdoors is where they find their voice.

The social and emotional skills are transferred into the classroom: "we've seen improvement in leadership qualities and imaginative skills. Now, they don't come to me if they can't get something to work or something is not going to plan."

Ashleigh felt it was important to consult parents, but she was also apprehensive: "Would parents just view it as 'they're just going outside to get muddy?'" However, the feedback was overwhelmingly positive:

Parents said that they picked up happier children on Ranger Days and they also reported improvements in concentration. They were able to have better discussions with their children at home because their children were actually listening. Pupils were more contented, and there was less desire to go on tablets and also less of: "I'm bored! What should I do?" Many parents commented that their children were making proper memories and that, on

the "Ranger Days," they were always able to remember and share what they'd done. After a few years of the Rangers approach, parents are now entirely on board with the school's approach to play and fully expect us to operate in that way now.

Historically, this community has suffered higher than average levels of deprivation, and reports state that there are still unacceptably high levels of child poverty. In one part of the local area, poverty affects almost

25% of children (Mcmurrich, 2019). Many pupils at the school don't have access to a garden or a big public outdoor space, and parents are grateful that the children get these play opportunities. Some of the children have had limited outdoor play experience, and some parents learned new ways to tune into their children's play.

Communication with parents has been key to the school's outdoor play journey:

> We established a dialogue with those parents who weren't as on board, and we discussed the benefits of this type of play. It's not just about getting muddy and messy, and it's not about making extra work for parents. It may look as though they are just rolling in mud, but actually they are exploring measure, they are building a bridge, they are talking about how to make it longer or shorter. There is a lot more going on. We do still occasionally get some people coming to us and saying "what's the real benefit of this? My daughter came home really muddy today." We are happy to sit down with them and explain the benefits. If you are open and you're honest, you're explaining the benefits of it to the parents, you are definitely less likely to get complaints. Part of our transition process is explaining to parents how we operate and how we learn through play. Our transition starts from February/March, so by the time they start in August, they are fully educated on what to expect when their child comes to school.

The school's outdoor play policy explains the benefits of their play approach in terms of mental health, wellbeing, and social and academic progress. "It's about giving parents the information before their child even starts school, so parents have a clear idea of the expectations and how things work." Parents are also invited to attend 'stay and play' sessions to see the benefits themselves, and Ashleigh regularly posts images and videos of outdoor play on social media to show how the children choose to play and how it helps them progress. "Parents love to see exactly what the children are doing, and they love the fact that the children are able to follow their own interests. We never get complaints that there is too much play going on."

Conclusion

Outdoor play can strengthen our partnership with parents, and parents often have invaluable skills, ideas, and resources to contribute. We have to put work into these relationships, and they can sometimes be problematic, but every child needs to feel that their family belongs.

TIME TO REFLECT:

- What would you like parents to better understand about your outdoor play provision?
- How do you communicate your outdoor play ethos to parents?
- How do you share outdoor play research with parents?
- How could you use outdoor play as a vehicle to engage marginalised parents?

References

Reading for children

Hoffman, M. and Asquith, R. (2015). *The Great Big Book of Families*. London: Frances Lincoln Children's Books.

Reading for adults

Garvey, D. (2018). *Nurturing Personal, Social and Emotional Development in Early Childhood: A Practical Guide to Understanding*

Brain Development and Young Children's Behaviour. London: Jessica Kingsley Publishers Ltd.

Gillespie, L. and Hunter, A. (2011). Creating healthy attachments to the babies in your care. *YC: Young Children*, 66(5), 62–63.

Goldschmied, E. and Selleck, D. (1996). *Communication between Babies in Their First Year, Video and Booklet*. London: National Children's Bureau.

Goodenow, C. (1993). Classroom belonging among early adolescent students: Relationships to motivation and achievement. *The Journal of Early Adolescence*, 13(1), 21–43. doi:10.1177/0272431693013001002

Mcmurrich, L. (2019). *North Lanarkshire Council Report Policy and Strategy Committee Approval Noting Local Child Poverty Action Report from Executive Summary*. [online] Available at: https://mars .northlanarkshire.gov.uk/egenda/images/att90955.pdf.

Parsons, K. and Traunter, J. (2020). Muddy knees and muddy needs: Parents' perceptions of outdoor learning. *Children's Geographies*, 18(6), 699–711. doi:10.1080/14733285.2019.1694637

Scott, S. (2004). *Fierce Conversations: Achieving Success at Work & in Life, One Conversation at a Time*. New York: Berkley Books.

Shonkoff, J.P. and Phillips, D.A. (eds). (2000). *From Neurons to Neighbourhoods: The Science of Early Childhood Development*. Washington, DC: National Academy Press.

Siegel, D.J. (2001). Toward an interpersonal neurobiology of the developing mind: Attachment relationships, *"mindsight,"* and neural integration. *Infant Mental Health Journal*, 22(1–2), 67–94.

Vandell, D. and Wilson, K. (1987). Infants' interactions with mother, sibling, and peer: contrasts and relations between interaction systems. *Child Development*, 58(1): 176–86.

Wheeler, H., Connor, J., Goodwin, H. and National Children's Bureau. (2009). *Parents, Early Years and Learning: Parents as Partners in the Early Years Foundation Stage; Principles into Practice*. London: National Children's Bureau.

Closing remarks

I'd like to leave the last word to a child. 'Jack' is a looked after child and the best part of any day for him is playing outdoors. 'Jack's' carer asked him what he needs to play...

I like to bounce,
I like to climb,
I like to do handstands,
I like to run and jump,
I like to scoot,
I like sand and stones and sticks and water,
I need a rope,
I need bats and balls, a tennis ball,
I need a big space, a tree to climb, a tyre to swing on,
I need other children to play with,
I need to play.

DOI: 10.4324/9781003137023-7

Index